What do parents say about *The Three P's?*

"The life planning ideas are so inspirational, and the book gives you simple, concrete steps to follow. We couldn't put it down. It's jam-packed with revelations about our kids...."
—Martha & Scott, parents of two girls, 11 and 14

"The section on timeouts is one we think every parent is going to remember...full of surprising insights."
—Jen & Art, parents of two boys, 4 and 6

"What a wakeup call! The responsibility chapter is a daily read for us. We saw an immediate change in our children."
—Anne & Jean-Claude, parents of three boys, 4, 12, and 15

"I wanted to rip out the page on 'relaxation discipline' and tape it up to read each day."
—Alina, mother of a 3-year-old girl

"The section on recess and aggression is a must-read. Takes you deep into your child's world, and makes you realize how little you know about your children."
—Brian and Yolanda, parents of a boy and girl, 8 and 14

"There are so many problems you can avoid as a parent by using the 'preemptive dialogue' technique. It's obvious stuff, but no one ever thinks to do it."
—Miriam, mother of two girls, 4 and 6

"Suddenly, you see the possibilities for an honest relationship with your child."
—Carolina and Will, parents of a girl and two boys, 10, 11 and 13

The Three P's of Parenting

The Three P's of Parenting

Jennifer Jones, Ph.D.

LearnGarden, Inc.
New York

learngarden

LearnGarden, Inc.
P.O. Box 1437
New York, NY 10274-1333

LearnGarden® is a registered trademark of LearnGarden, Inc.

Library of Congress Cataloging-In-Publication Data

Jones, Jennifer (Jennifer L.)
The Three P's of Parenting / by Jennifer
Jones, Ph.D.---LearnGarden, Inc.

p. cm.
ISBN 978-1-4243-3313-4 (pbk.)
Pending CIP categories

LearnGarden books are available for special promotions and
premiums.

First published in 2007 by LearnGarden, Inc.

Printed in the United States of America
10 9 8 7 6 5 4 3 2 1

For

My mother
and evolving parents everywhere

CONTENTS

Ms. Yvonne's Classroom

"Pretty soon, you will see their masterpieces," said Yvonne Smith, master teacher of 30 years, whose reputation as a "child whisperer" had led me, a decade ago, to her classroom in New York's East Harlem neighborhood. We stood looking at the freshly wet paintings, the first creations of the year by her four- and five-year-old students. I stared in disbelief at the sheets of mucky brown blobs and retorted, "These kids are a long way from making masterpieces."

I was wrong.

In less than a month, every child in Yvonne's classroom produced sophisticated works of artistic integrity. Children I thought were incapable of even cleaning their own brushes were rendering brilliant figurative and abstract expressions of landscapes, people, and experiences. They mixed colors with care, thought and vision, generating their own palettes to express the rich imagery of their thoughts.

How did Yvonne extract such talent from these tots? With modeling and coaching. She began by gathering the children in a circle the day after the "brown blobs" had been hung. She did not say a word. She sat cross- legged on the floor, her imposing figure, salt-and-pepper dreadlocks, and billowing bohemian skirt making her look like Mother Earth herself.

She laid in front of her the tools of the art process: brushes, water, sponge, mixing tray, containers of paint in primary colors. The children huddled in quiet expectation. Yvonne moved slowly and methodically as she placed her paints on her mixing tray. She held up her brush. She dipped it in yellow. She placed the yellow on her tray. She held up her brush again. The children tittered with nervous excitement but dared not move.

Yvonne dipped her brush in the water and swished it about. This water play captivated her students, and their excitement mounted, but still no one budged. Yvonne dried her brush and repeated the process with other colors, pausing for long moments to allow her students to absorb the lesson. As her yellow turned green, and then chartreuse, the children marveled. Yvonne was modeling.

Yvonne repeated this lesson several times in the following days, each time expanding it with increasingly advanced painting procedures. As children attempted her techniques, she encouraged them to take chances and to think for themselves. Yvonne was coaching.

By month's end, the children not only cleaned their own brushes, but maintained the entire art center, its stock, order and use. Children who could not yet spell "art" exhibited a maturity of participation in this system that shocked me. This was not a gifted classroom. These were ordinary children from a range of socio-economic backgrounds.

And that is not all. By the end of the year, the children were managing their own classroom—a large, materials-rich series of learning centers focusing on math, science, reading, sculpture, craft, architecture and role-play. These young children managed it all, and even managed their own movements in and out of the classroom. All of this was a result of Yvonne's modeling and coaching. She rarely spoke. She never raised her voice. And her classroom was the epitome of harmony and collaboration.

The experience in Ms. Yvonne's classroom prompted me to devote the past decade to exploring the behaviors of children and the relationships they have with adults. I came to know and work with hundreds of children and families from every walk of life, and observed some universal patterns in child behavior and in the way parents respond to that behavior. Inspired by the practices of some visionary parents, I discovered a host of simple, straightforward strategies for achieving harmony in the parent-child relationship. It is the excitement of these discoveries and the promise of their untapped potential that has led me to share my findings with you.

Introduction
Origin of The Three P's

Childhood has a delicate side that we all want to nurture and protect. The imaginative spirit of children, their tenderness, and their unbridled sincerity all bring us joy, give us meaning, and offer us a glimpse of ourselves as we once were, before life and its trials hardened us. So, we protect children to preserve that delicate side and to prolong their contentment, and ours.

However, in protecting the cherished elements of childhood, there is a tendency to overlook an important side of a child's experience, one that is less ethereal and more rooted in uncertainty. Psychologists are acquainted with this darker side of a child's experience because it is the source of so many of the unresolved emotional issues for which we seek closure as adults. In the less visible experience of childhood, we each grappled in quiet worry with a feeling of helplessness, a fear of abandonment, and a fear of the unknown.

Children naturally feel helpless, because they are. They do not have money, keys, phones, cars, or words to communicate their needs. They are physically limited in height, strength and mobility, and they know it. They watch you take the lid off of a jar, but they cannot; when they go to open the door, the handle is out of reach; the ball you catch so easily hits them in the face. And children recognize their predicament. In some respects, their experience is similar to that of the elderly; there is dependence on others for nearly everything and frustration when their needs are not met or understood.

It is also natural for children to fear abandonment. Should something happen to us, or should we stop loving them, children know instinctively that they are in big trouble because they depend on us for everything. Consequently, until children feel physically and mentally prepared to navigate the world around them independently, they stay carefully attuned to their protectors, watching for any signs that their survival is in jeopardy.

Finally, children fear the unknown because it is all around them, with potential dangers lurking everywhere. This is why children are transfixed by television and movies, particularly when the content is violent. For them, news or visual stories hold information about the complex world "out there" and how one should prepare for it. The more we try to conceal this information, the more valuable it is to them. Their desire to know what lies ahead is a subconscious one, driven by intelligent survival instincts.

Children are not able to articulate these feelings of uncertainty, fear or helplessness, and so parents are often unaware of this darker side of a child's experience. Instead of using words, the child communicates his needs and insecurities through behavioral "signals."

These signals start at infancy, when your newborn summons you with cries to attend to his needs. He then continues, throughout his life, to signal his needs with his behavior, employing increasingly sophisticated techniques over time.

Most parents, however, are programmed to view behavior in terms of defiance or compliance. So when a child throws a tantrum, refuses to be potty-trained, rejects dinner, pushes his little brother, forgets to do his homework, comes home late, tries drugs or gets a tattoo, parents are likely to react to the visible behavior by treating it as defiance, without understanding the motivation behind it. The child's motivation is to satisfy a need, and there are three key needs that every child has and that every parent should learn to recognize.

WHAT ARE THE THREE P'S?

Every child needs "The Three P's," and if you provide them, you will have a happy child and a harmonious relationship with him. The "P's" are: power, protection, and prediction.

"Power" is what your child feels when he can make decisions or participate in those that impact him. "Protection" is what gives him confidence that his basic needs will be met and that he is prepared for the challenges he will face. "Prediction" is your child's certainty about the future and his sense that he can rely on your word.

Your child's behavior is his way of signaling you about his need for one or more of these P's. You can have a remarkable parent-child relationship for the life of your child by learning to recognize his signals and know when the P's are lacking. It is that simple, and it applies to your infant, toddler, tween, and teen.

Why these particular P's? Because they each correspond with the major insecurities that plague children—feeling helpless, fearing abandonment, and worrying about the unknown. Each of these elements of a child's "darker" world are addressed by provision of the P's.

When a child lacks *power*, he feels helpless, so he will assert himself or try to control others. When a child feels *unprotected*, he will draw others near with attention-getting actions. When a child cannot *predict* what will happen or what those around him will do, he will focus his energy on controlling the behavior and responses of others so that his world feels more certain.

Behavior is your child's way of telling you that he has a need, and that need generally falls within the realm of one or more of the P's.

Parenting Today

Why, if these truths are so simple, are they not part of today's parenting lexicon?

First, parenting has long been a practice driven by tradition, as each generation encourages the next to adhere to an established set of views on children and their rearing. Because parenting plays such an important role in the preservation of culture, new parents can find it difficult to maintain tradition while challenging the family's assumptions about children. As a result, a family's rationale for its approach to discipline or explanations for a child's behavior can become part of the legend that passes unchallenged from one generation to the next.

Second, analysis and probing of the parent-child relationship has historically been the domain of "experts" such as psychologists and learning specialists, who have the benefit of universal experience with children but lack that critical advantage of knowing *your* child day in and day out. In essence, the parent has been left out of the most important conversations about children and given the least amount of formal training, yet is the first to be blamed when the child goes awry.

Lastly, the inner life of a child—his motivations, fears and preoccupations—is hidden from his parents. A child cannot articulate what he feels and why, so it is up to us to decipher his behavior and address his needs proactively.

WHEN TO USE THIS BOOK

When is it too late to address those needs? Never. All that changes as your child ages are the strategies that you use. Are you too late if your child is 8 or 9? 15 or 16? Already in his twenties? Absolutely not. Learning how to read your child's signals and understand his true motivation can help you at any stage of his life, even into adulthood.

Each part of this book deals with one of the P's, providing examples of the signals children send when they are lacking a particular P, what those signals mean and how to respond to them and even prevent them.

I have been careful to provide suggestions that are appropriate for all age groups, with minor tweaking to make them developmentally right for your child. Each chapter includes age-specific tips to help you develop an approach that suits your situation best.

REAL PRACTICES FROM TRUE VISIONARIES

Throughout this book, you will find case studies and

examples in which some of the most common parenting problems are addressed with practices that may, at first, seem strange. You may find yourself dismissing them as impractical or impossible. Yet, everything in this book is taken from actual parenting experiences, and every strategy suggested has been used by a real parent to solve (or prevent) a problem you have faced or are likely to encounter.

It is because these innovative approaches are so rare that I have endeavored to share them with you here. Parenting is often a practice we learn based on the models we see around us, and we sometimes take for granted that the parent-child relationships we see represent the limit of what is possible. Plus, because raising children is as much a social experience as it is a private one, it can be challenging to use innovative techniques when others around you do not.

If you have been parenting for a few years, you may simply have grown accustomed to your child's behavior and become less conscious of the everyday decisions you make and how they impact him. Your interactions may now form a routine that has become part of the fabric of your relationship, and so even dissonance between you may seem normal and unchangeable.

But if you embrace the idea of visionary parenting, of building a relationship with your child based not on what you see around you but on what you *want* to have, you will find affirmation here in the stories of others like you who have achieved such visions.

As you read the following pages, you may gain perspective that triggers concern about your parenting approach or doubts about whether you have made the right decisions. However, nothing contained in this book represents a critique of your approach. If you are reading this book, you are already an effective parent, because you are taking thoughtful action in the interest of your child's well-being.

This book was written not to judge your parenting, but to help you understand the motivations and inner workings of your child so that you can recognize the signals he is sending you, understand what they mean and know how to respond. As you better understand your child, you will find yourself feeling more confident in addressing any problem that childrearing brings, relying not on guesswork, but on your informed instinct.

Use this book as a pathway to becoming more powerful as a parent, more confident about your decisions and closer to your child. You are the person best positioned to advocate for your child's success and happiness. All you need are the right tools. So, let's begin.

Part One

Power

Chapter One
Why Children Seek Power

From the time we are born, we all want to feel control over what we do and what happens to us. Babies may be born helpless, but they instinctively know how to secure milk, hold the parent's gaze, and find relief from a wet diaper. They learn quickly to get what they want through cries of varying tonalities, and nature has given them strong lungs to register their needs. We respond on cue.

Thus, from the cradle, children are attuned to the dynamics of power and control, and are constantly testing this through both positive and negative behaviors. An infant screams, a toddler throws a tantrum, an eight-year-old refuses dinner, and a teen comes home ridiculously late, all to test power. What power? The power to control you (because you control everything else) and to be independent from you.

The less adversarial power-seeking takes the form of pleasing behavior. When your child pleases you, he feels loved, which, for him, equates with devotion and protection. Because children depend on us so completely, securing our devotion is critical. For that reason, an infant may test his power to please you by smiling back at you, the toddler by learning to recognize new words, the fourth grader by cleaning his room, and the teen by making it home before curfew. Does your child behave well only to please you, with no other purpose than to secure your devotion? Of course not, but as long as he is dependent on you, pleasing you is of utmost importance because your devotion directly impacts his feelings of security and stability.

The power play that we begin as children continues into adulthood. In adult life, we are constantly testing and negotiating power. At the workplace, with our friends, with our family and in romantic relationships, we strive to please and secure the devotion of others, exercise our independence, and look for ways to control outcomes. So, while it may seem strange to think of power in association with our children, it plays an important role in their lives, just as it does in ours.

DOES YOUR CHILD HAVE POWER?

Children seek power because they have so little, and because instinct compels them to become more capable, self-sufficient and mature. Accordingly, children of all ages eagerly seek more complex challenges and become frustrated when freedom and opportunity fall short of their readiness.

Before we go further, I would like to address a common concern among parents. Many worry that empowering their children will involve yielding authority to their children or permitting them to make decisions that they are not prepared to make. On the contrary, a child cannot be empowered or feel stable without clear parental authority and leadership, and it is that leadership that will ultimately serve as a model for him. So when I suggest that your child needs power in order to fulfill his call to maturity, I am not suggesting that he *over*power you in the process.

Now, take a moment to think through your child's day (best done for children ages 2-18). Reflect on the ways in which he is expected to make decisions, to control his physical environment, and to try new skills. Starting with the beginning of the day, picture the routines that constitute the morning, day and evening. What power does your child have in each phase of his day? What decisions is he allowed to make on his own? What physical control does he have over his activity? How much do you trust him to make choices? And, most importantly, how have you coached him in making those choices?

To help you, I have listed below the activities that most of us perform on a daily basis. How many of these activities does your child do for himself? How many do you do for him? Use this list to evaluate how much power your child experiences in the everyday moments of his life.

If you have a young child, you may feel that he is too young to accomplish these tasks on his own, or perhaps you enjoy doing them for him. If you have a tween or teen, you may envision him shirking some of these tasks or handling them irresponsibly.

If you are having these reactions, I ask that you put your reservations aside for now, and keep your visionary mind active as we further explore the process of inviting a child to have and manage power. You may be surprised to discover the impact that simple everyday tasks can have on your child's self-esteem and maturity, and ultimately on your relationship with him.

EVERYDAY TASKS

MORNING

- waking up at a set time
- completing morning hygiene
- dressing properly for the day
- making the bed
- preparing/eating breakfast

DAILY ACTIVITY

- preparing/eating snacks or light meals
- completing tasks/chores
- choosing entertainment
- engaging in hobbies or personal interests
- exercising

BEDTIME

- recognizing a set bedtime
- dressing for bed and bedtime hygiene
- engaging in calming activities prior to sleep

Before reading on, mentally give your child a "power score" from 1 to 10, where 10 equates with having control of most of his everyday experiences and 1 equates with having little. Keep this score in mind as we explore the signals children use when they feel a lack of power. You may find that there is a direct correlation between your child's power score and the behaviors described below.

THE SIGNALS

Children are constantly communicating their need for power, but we can miss their signals if we react to the behavior too quickly without taking the time to observe what they are doing. Your child sends power signals in a variety of forms, driven primarily by his Age-Stage Priorities and his relationship with you.

AGE-STAGE PRIORITIES

I am not the first, and I will certainly not be the last, to define children by stages. However, I find most descriptions of a child's development overly technical and confusing for the layperson. Here is a simple breakdown explaining what your child cares about most in each of the three basic phases of youth. These guidelines will be useful as we explore how your child signals that he has these needs.

Wobbly Age: Your child wants nurturing and physical challenges.

Lunchbox Age: He wants to be as much like you (or your spouse or partner) as possible, build intellectual skills, and attempt increasingly difficult tasks.

Telephone Age: He wants to be attractive to others (not just physically), to have gradual independence from you, and to affiliate with a group or cause.

For **Wobbly Age** children, most power signals come in physical form because those are the skills your child instinctively seeks to develop first. As he begins to roll over, pull himself up, and struggle in your arms, the pursuit of power is on.

Many of us have forgotten the thrill and exhilaration of learning to walk, run, jump, and climb for the first time. To take a step and have it result in a predictable outcome is nothing short of astounding for your toddler. Each physical task he conquers fuels a desire for more, and children between the ages of two and four experience a sense of unparalleled vitality and potential.

But your toddler's enthusiasm for a challenge is inversely proportional to yours. Freeze-frame your reaction to his first attempts to walk down stairs, run ahead of you toward the street, climb onto a stool to reach a high shelf, swim toward the deep end. What do you feel? Panic? Fear? Anxiety? These are what I call "signs of discord."

Your child sees every nuance of your reaction to his boldness. He sees the fear in your eyes, the tension in your face, and the lurch of your body, and he logs that information. If he behaves in a way that provokes these reactions in you, he is signaling you.

What does the signal mean? It means that your child is seeking one or more of the three P's, and in this particular case, he is most likely seeking power. How do you know? Because he is attempting new physical feats that give him a rush of adrenaline (notice the look of excitement on his face?).

However, because he is of **Wobbly Age**, he is not comfortable trying new physical challenges without the reassurance of your watchful eye. He knows that when he takes a risk, you will come nearer, out of fear, and this is what he wants. He wants more power, but he wants to feel protected by you as he experiments with it. By testing your behaviors, he has discovered that flirting with danger is a way to get the results he wants.

If your **Wobbly Age** child is exhibiting this type of behavior, then the everyday opportunities for power you are currently providing may not match the level of capability he senses in himself. Increase his exposure to structured physical challenges and training, and he will stop trying to trigger your fear through dangerous pursuits.

To prevent **Wobbly Age** children from trying dangerous physical feats, provide as much opportunity for structured physical challenge as possible between the ages of 2 and 4. Classes that teach physical control—such as those in gymnastics or dance—and toys that can be used to practice control—like those found at Leaps and Bounds® (www.leapsandbounds.com) or Lakeshore Learning's "active play" department (www.lakeshorelearning.com)—will discourage a **Wobbly Age** child from doing things to make you fearful.

Once children gain a certain degree of control over their bodies, you will notice that their language skills kick into high gear. They will use "hot button" words or phrases to get your attention because your shocked reaction makes them feel powerful.

Children of **Lunchbox Age** may use power signals associated with skill development and mimicking. For example, a child that age may impersonate your parenting behaviors, attempt household chores, or work tenaciously on his handwriting. Because your **Lunchbox Age** child feels himself growing more capable at ever-increasing rates, and because he wants so desperately to be like you (or an older sibling), he is likely to become frustrated or exasperated ("I can't do it!") with skills of precision associated with school or sports. If he does not have adequate opportunity to exercise power (skill development) at this age, you might find him outwardly defiant of you, or increasingly passive-aggressive as he ignores, forgets or "doesn't hear" your instructions. These are ways he has found to exert power in the absence of more constructive options.

You know your child is seeking power when you feel like giving up or giving in.

Whether positive or negative, power signals are always tied to the priorities of the child in his particular phase of youth. In the **Lunchbox Age**, most of his positive power signals will take the form of pleasing you with his achievements. His negative power signals will make you feel like giving in to his desires or giving up on what you have asked him to do.

> To prevent **Lunchbox Age** children from seeking power in negative ways, provide safe, nurturing, but structured opportunities for them to learn skills of precision, such as those related to sports, the arts, computers, and writing. They will be particularly responsive to learning any skills that you use on a daily basis, including cleaning, home repairs, gardening, cooking, or use of electronics.

For children of **Telephone Age**, power signals are tied primarily to your child's social experiences. Because being liked by others equates with power for him, most of his behavior will be toward social ends. So, he may alter his appearance and mannerisms for peer approval or ask for things or privileges that his peers promote. Like the **Lunchbox Age** child, if your tween or teen lacks adequate opportunity to feel constructive power, he is likely to become destructive by defying your authority or using subterfuge to undermine it, which is why power-poor teens are known to lie or conceal the truth and "forget" important messages or deadlines, especially those related to school.

As I have mentioned, there is a "pleasing" behavior that children use when seeking power. Some **Telephone Age** children will seek to please through superlative achievement, usually directed at peers, but occasionally at their parents. Your child may work to become the most popular, most attractive, friendliest or most intelligent student among his peers, although he will not necessarily choose peer groups you like. If he has a sibling, he may attempt to master a skill his sibling cannot. Whatever helps him gain dominance, approval or acceptance translates into power.

> To prevent **Telephone Age** children from seeking power in negative ways, provide and encourage highly involved, challenging and mature opportunities for group involvement in a cause, initiative, or project. He will respond positively to anything that involves social engagement (for shy teens, this means online) and identity development. Aim for activities that involve making a difference (environmental protection), long-term projects (small business venture), or team achievement (sports, dance, debate). These promote personal accountability and life direction. Above all, seek opportunities for him to have meaningful and structured responsibility (i.e., title, role, project leadership, etc.) within a group.

On the next page, I have provided a basic code for how your child may behave when power is lacking. As you can see, the most common behaviors are: control, challenging authority, sabotage, aggression and seeking acceptance. Let us take a look at the last two, because in order to address them as a parent, you will need to understand the hidden dynamic involved in each.

Aggression. When your child attacks you or someone else, especially if it is a physical attack, it is usually with a feeling of fear or insecurity. When he first strikes out, he feels a momentary rush of power. However, that feeling quickly subsides when he realizes what he has done, and he plummets back into the fear and insecurity that prompted him to be aggressive in the first place.

Once your child has acted on this feeling, aggression can become addictive. He will be attracted to the "high" of physically dominating someone because he feels powerless in his own life, and so he may become aggressive more frequently to avoid experiencing the "low" of insecurity that haunts him when he is not on the attack.

Behavior	What It Looks Like
Control	He makes you do what he wants you to do. For example, telling on his sister so that you scold her or interrupting your phone call so that you end it early.
Challenge to Authority	He defies your rules. For example, refusing to go to bed on time or getting a nose piercing.
Sabotage	He fails to act so that your power is undermined. For example, he loses homework, forgets to clean his room, or fails to tell you about an important deadline.
Aggressing Others	He bullies another child verbally or physically, or physically attacks you.
Seeking Acceptance	He seeks your approval or that of his peers. For example, he constantly shows you his drawings or school work, or he is obsessively uncertain about whether he is liked by his peers.

Seeking Acceptance. There is also a hidden dynamic when your child seeks acceptance in a peer group. Children seek power through affiliation, just as we do. The more powerless a tween or teen feels, the more desperate he will be for this type of affiliation, and the less scrutinizing he will be about the moral code of that group.

For example, a teen who tries to join a group of high-achieving students, but is rejected, will shift his priorities to gain acceptance by another group, even if that means sabotaging his academic performance. He wants to belong much more than he wants to be great.

Furthermore, if you do not provide him with power, and you get in the way of his acceptance, he will defy you before he will defy the group that embraces him.

POWER AND MISBEHAVIOR

We only test power when we are uncertain of it. Adults who feel secure in love and work seldom seek attention or conflict. When we do something negative to ourselves or to others, we do so because we are lacking something—power, self-confidence, basic needs, love. Children are the same; they only commit misbehavior when they have an unmet need.

Most parents react to this type of power-seeking behavior with suppression, restraint, limitations, and force. Certainly these are instinctive responses, and naturally you want to discourage destructive behavior; but over the longer term, does it make sense to respond to a child's need for power with suppression of that power?

Power is the carrot that advances the child's maturity, encouraging a more sophisticated command of the world around him. To deny him power is to discourage his growth.

Your child wants to know, experience, and become competent in your world. He is biologically programmed to want this. He is curious about the attention you give to your world. You are the model of survival and existence for him, and whatever you do with your time is something he also wants to do. He lives in constant awe and appreciation of your power; if he challenges it, he is probably seeking his rightful share.

In the next chapter, we take a deeper look at the relationship between power and misbehavior, what motivates your child to misbehave, how you typically respond to that behavior, and why you might not be getting the results you want from the disciplinary methods you are using.

Chapter Two
Power and Discipline

We have established why your child wants power and how she signals her need for it. Now we are going to look at how you react to her power-seeking behavior and the cycle that takes shape as a result.

The Logic of Misbehavior

You may think you are disciplining your child, but are you really? If you react to her behavior by applying rules of right and wrong, governed by your view of what is appropriate, then you are not disciplining her; she is disciplining you.

How is this possible? Because we are using adult logic in a child's game. Children do not define behavior or relationships quite the way we do. They see the world from a different perspective because of their dependency on us. They are constantly testing our attentiveness and ability to provide, because their survival depends on it. So, from the start, they are more attuned to our behavioral patterns than we are to theirs. On top of that, because they operate from a motive of survival, they are less concerned with "right and wrong" and more concerned with their security and stability (i.e., survival).

Therefore, in your child's world, behavior is right if it makes her life more predictable, makes her stronger, or makes you more attentive. In her mind, behavior is wrong if it increases her uncertainty or her exposure to harm.

From birth, your child began forming conclusions about your rules, using her keen powers of observation and hearing. Even as an infant, she sensed what would elicit your smile and what would elicit your frown. She observed the nuances in your body language, heard the subtle variations in the pitch and tone of your voice, and logged your actions and reactions to her and to others, all for the purpose of understanding what pleases you and what does not. By the **Wobbly Age**, after careful observation of you—and at least one test—your child knows how you will react to most behaviors.

So, if your child misbehaves, it is not because she has forgotten the rules, but because with misbehavior she has a better chance of getting her needs met. Subconsciously, she wants your reaction, or she would not behave that way in the first place.

Herein lies the problem. The standard parenting approach is to wait for misbehavior and then react to it. Therefore, it is usually in the best interest of your child to actively seek fulfillment of her needs with whatever behavior gets your attention the quickest and most reliably, even if it upsets you, rather than wait indefinitely for you to realize that her need exists.

This is why most adult reactions to a child's misbehavior often do little more than reinforce it. When you think you are reprimanding or punishing your child, you may merely be responding to programming she has learned to use to make you more attentive or reliable. In a way, she is driving the parenting.

For instance, a child of **Lunchbox Age** wanted power, so she let her mother know by coaxing the father to let her stay up late on a school night, even though the mother had strictly forbidden it. She knew the mother would be frustrated when she found out that her ruling had been overturned, and she knew that there was little the mother could do about it. She expected the mother to become angry and to argue with the father, and she expected to be punished. But in the end, she got what she wanted: a sense of power and control, not to mention undivided attention from both parents.

A child of **Telephone Age** wanted power, so she let her parents know by demanding a cell phone based on the fact that each of her friends had one. Because she was approaching her parents confrontationally, she had already anticipated that they would refuse her demands (which they did), and she built a case against them as unfair parents. In doing so, she leveraged the power of her friends against them, because it was her association with her friends that was giving her the sensation of power.

In each instance, the behavior was meant to cause a specific reaction in the parents, and that reaction—be it tough or tender—was exactly what the child was seeking from the start.

> To know the true motivation for your child's behavior, look for the end result she achieves with it.

Your Reaction is the Driver

While your child's logic may sound complicated, it is actually quite simple. To decipher her intent, follow the trail of your interaction, starting with how that behavior makes you feel and ending with the outcome of the interaction. If her behavior upsets you to the point of giving up, then you are relinquishing power and distancing yourself emotionally and even physically. She is pushing you away so that she can feel more powerful.

To better understand this dynamic, let us compare it to what happens when your child wants one of the other P's, protection. If she pushes you away to get power, then she will pull you closer to get protection. For example, if her behavior ignites your rage and, as a result, you get physically closer and give her attention, it does not matter that you are upset, because you are giving her what she was seeking, your focus and your closeness.

On the chart below you will see a comparison of four feelings that you are likely to have in response to your child's behavior and what those feelings reveal about her intent.

How your child's behavior makes you feel	How you look to your child	What your reaction means to your child	What your child may be seeking
Angry	Fierce Powerful Dominant	You are in control and can protect her.	Protection
Fearful	Attentive Protective	You will protect her.	Protection
Frustrated	Weak Defeated	You will give up.	Power
Disappointed	Detached	You are releasing control.	Power

Do you see a pattern? A child who wants protection will provoke you to be fierce or attentive. A child who wants power will make you give in, give up or get some distance.

POWER-PLUS-PROTECTION

Because there is a close relationship between power and protection, let me pause to clarify how they play a dual role in the way that your child attempts to program you. I address protection as an isolated motive in greater depth in Part Two.

The need for power and the need for protection are not mutually exclusive. Sometimes, your child seeks them as a package.

You may remember the adventurous toddler I described earlier, the one who runs ahead of you, climbs up to cabinets, and swims into deep water. In each of these daring acts, the **Wobbly Age** child seeks power (through challenge) and protection (through your attention). This pattern continues through each phase of youth, as children seek the power to grow and become independent *while* securing the protection they need to explore new and sometimes daunting experiences.

Your **Lunchbox Age** child might seek power-plus-protection with incessant calls of "Watch me! Watch me!" to capture your attention while showing off a new skill, or she might harass a sibling until you intervene, and then convince you to endorse her behavior.

Teens of **Telephone Age** seek the power-protection combination with social behaviors, such as dressing provocatively, smoking or hanging out with groups whose values contradict yours. Behaviors like these are experiments with power, but they also stimulate your protectiveness, which your teen secretly wants, even though she may complain about it to her friends.

What do these examples demonstrate? That in most cases, the reaction you have to your child's behavior satisfies the need she was trying to fill, even if that reaction is an angry or disappointed one. She is not averse to making you upset, as long as doing so satisfies her need for one or more of the three P's.

So, should you continue disciplining or punishing your child? Yes, of course, until you are able to satisfy her needs proactively rather than reactively. Should you have to discipline her? No, because she already knows how you would like her to behave. In fact, she probably knows your expectations better than you know them yourself, because she has probably spent more time and taken more care to study your patterns than you have. After all, despite how her behavior may sometimes make you feel, she is still your biggest fan.

THE PROBLEM WITH TIMEOUTS

Many parenting guides recommend the use of timeouts for correcting a child's misbehavior. Timeouts, groundings, and "go to your room" penalties are ways to assert your power over your child and can be a quick fix for volatile situations. But using what we understand about the dynamics of discipline, let us examine what really happens when these methods are applied.

With children of **Wobbly Age** or **Lunchbox Age**, a parent will usually employ a timeout method based on the logic that isolation of the child will calm the behavior, calm the parent, and punish the child for wrongdoing. The parent often believes that isolation is something the child does not want. However, if you have used the timeout in response to the same behavior more than once, or if you have used it in response to numerous behaviors, your child has already learned how to program you to give this punishment. If the timeout was truly punitive for the child, she would not have misbehaved. Your child knows the rules. But more importantly, she knows you.

Some children program their parents to give the timeout because they enjoy the zen-like calm and escape from stress that the experience offers. However, most children program their parents to give the timeout for one of two reasons: 1) to receive more attention from the parent, or 2) to have distance from the parent's control. The difference lies in how the timeout is implemented.

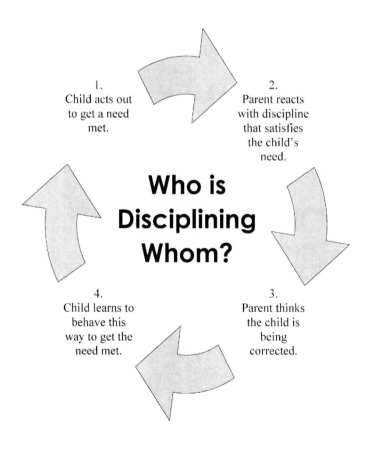

1.
Child acts out
to get a need
met.

2.
Parent reacts
with discipline
that satisfies
the child's
need.

**Who is
Disciplining
Whom?**

4.
Child learns to
behave this
way to get the
need met.

3.
Parent thinks
the child is
being
corrected.

Some parents attempt to isolate the child, but the child resists and ends up receiving more attention in the punishment than from the misbehavior that prompted it. Often, the struggle to enforce a timeout will end in exhaustion, which usually leads to softness and nurturing behavior by both parent and child. This end result of closeness is what the child was originally seeking. She knows it will come, eventually.

Some parents do succeed in isolating a child with timeouts, and those parents will often remark on how compliant the child is in response. These parents will say "She loves timeout so much that she sometimes puts herself in it." Indeed, she does love it, because it makes her feel powerful, both because her parents adore her for complying and because it distances them and gives her a vacation from what is probably a controlling environment.

With children of **Telephone Age**, parents often resort to grounding (the more sophisticated version of timeout). Isolation from social activity can indeed be torturous for a tween or teen, but if you have used grounding more than once, then your child has learned how to be grounded, and is most likely programming you to use this technique. Why would a teen *seek* to be grounded? The answer lies in how your child responds to this form of punishment. A teen who resists wants to challenge your power because she lacks her own; she needs something to push against.

A teen who readily complies with grounding may feel unsafe in her social setting and is seeking safe harbor in the isolation you are imposing on her. She cannot afford to bow out of social experiences, as that would be "uncool," so she provokes you and then portrays you to her friends as the villain.

So, while there is nothing inherently wrong with timeouts or groundings, they probably do not address the problem you are targeting, and they do not promote a constructive relationship between you and your child. Timeouts and groundings perpetuate the power- and attention-seeking behaviors that prompted them in the first place, and do not promote trust, communication, or your child's maturity.

THE POWER OF PRIVACY

One approach to discipline that does allow you to correct behavior without disempowering your child, yields instant results and helps you build a parent-child bond, is privacy. Privacy is a quiet form of discipline, and goes unnoticed by those around you. You are giving your child privacy when you whisper a firm reminder in her ear, so that she is not publicly humiliated by your admonishment, or when you remove your child from onlookers before you tell her your concerns.

Remember how embarrassed you were when scolded in front of others? You could not look beyond your own embarrassment to see the lesson you were being given. That humiliation can quickly turn into resentment and internalized anger, which breeds and manifests itself in passive-aggressive acts, such as when your child refuses to eat, delays you when you are in a rush, or fails to perform academically.

Disciplining in private is particularly important when parenting siblings, because they live in close quarters with a delicate power balance. Reprimanding one child in front of the others fuels their power struggle, or encourages all of your children to unite against you in behavioral mutiny.

To avoid those pitfalls, try giving quiet reminders that exist as "secrets" between you and your child; this will make her feel respected and protected. She is more likely to comply with your direction when no one else knows you have given it because she does not have to prove to others that she has power. Providing her with a shield of privacy, while administering the discipline you feel is necessary, brings your child into the fold of your protection while coaching her toward your expectations.

A PROACTIVE APPROACH

While disciplining in private can accomplish a great deal in mitigating your child's misbehavior and building your relationship, it is still reactive parenting and, alone, is not enough to break the cycle of programming that your child has established.

You will be more effective in achieving the harmony you seek with your child when you use a proactive approach, providing for her needs before she is moved to misbehave. In essence, a proactive approach to parenting is a way of turning the tables so that instead of being programmed by your child, you are doing the programming, neutralizing her misbehavior and building a solid, nurturing relationship.

While proactive parenting is not the norm, it is a practice that exists in every corner of the world, and it is a practice compatible with every culture, socio-economic status, religion and political view. All of the proactive strategies this book provides are practiced by families whose visionary solutions were prompted by the same frustrations with child behavior that you, no doubt, have experienced.

You may have examples around you and not realize it. Look closely at the children who seem to be in harmony with their parents; you will see that those children have power. They are invited and expected to learn ever more challenging skills, they share in the important responsibilities of the household, and they derive power and privilege from their parents so that they are less inclined to seek it from peer groups.

HOW TO EVALUATE YOUR CHILD'S BEHAVIOR

The first step in moving from being a reactionary parent to a proactive parent is identifying your child's behaviors and their probable causes. If you have a spouse, each of you should do this process separately, and then compare notes. Most likely, your child is triggering each of you in different ways.

- List five examples of negative behaviors your child has demonstrated recently. Try to list unique examples.

- Describe how you reacted to each behavior. Think about your physical and emotional reactions. Did you look weak or strong? Did you give more attention or less?

- Jot down possible motivations for each behavior. Why did your child seek that reaction from you?

- Describe the outcome. How did it end? What did your child get as a result? Attention? Freedom? Victory? Isolation?

Once you have completed this reflection and compared notes with your spouse (and perhaps with others who provide care for your child), you are ready to begin de-programming your behavior and that of your child by preparing a course of "proaction" and opportunities for constructive empowerment.

The preventive effect of this approach cannot be overstated. Having power at a young age can transform a child and quell much of the rebellion that parents fear and dread. The Terrible Two's are not so terrible if the child has already been invited to take control of her body and many of her experiences. The preteen and teen years are not such a battleground if the child has already experienced multiple opportunities to execute and manage real responsibility.

Do not believe those who say that teens are naturally defiant. I know hundreds who are not, because they were empowered at a young age by parents who did not fear children with confidence and determination.

In fact, what some refer to as the natural rebellion of teenagers is actually the product of a teen's sense of powerlessness mixed with resentment toward the parent. A controlling parent responds to this rebellion with increased fear and a compulsion to "lock down," which launches the relationship into a hopeless power struggle in which parents and children both lose.

It does not have to be this way.

How to Discipline Proactively

In Chapter One, I listed a few of the most common behaviors used by children who lack power. Now that we have a better understanding of the traditional discipline-power dynamic, let us look at how a proactive parent might address these behaviors. We will review general approaches here and then go into more depth in the next chapter.

Control. Your child feels that one or more key aspects of her life is out of control. This is often true for children who are experiencing a divorce, a move, less time with a parent than usual, or intimidation by a bully or sibling.

As a proactive parent, first assess your child's situation, looking for factors that may make her feel vulnerable, uncertain, or unable to rely on you. Then introduce more reliability on your part (making a commitment and keeping it) and invite her to take control of more aspects of her life (through everyday tasks).

Challenging Authority. Your child feels capable, but she does not have adequate or suitable opportunities to demonstrate what she can do. She is a captain without a ship, so look for ways to enlist her in activities that are truly challenging for her, but still within your comfort zone. She might also be uncertain about your leadership, especially if you are experiencing a low point in your life. If this is the case, add togetherness time to your weekly schedule and give her your undivided attention, even if only for a few minutes. She will find this reassuring.

Sabotage. Your child is using passive-aggressive strategies to make you work harder (such as leaving messes for you to clean up), slow you down (such as making you late for work), or keep you out of the loop (such as "forgetting" key school information). She has not been expected or empowered to make decisions for herself or to deal with consequences when she does, but she wants this power. As a proactive parent, begin introducing increasingly critical decision-making opportunities for your child, tiering them so that with each success, she can aspire to higher goals.

Aggressing Other Children. Your child feels deeply insecure and intimidated by other children. If she has used aggression more than once, she may also be experiencing an addictive response to the rush of adrenaline and power she feels when she attacks others (discussed in Chapter One). As a proactive parent, nourish her self-esteem by identifying her strengths and providing opportunities for her to build skill in those areas. Then role-play aggression-related situations with her, each of you alternating roles so that she has a safe harbor for evaluating perspectives, thinking about her reactions and inventing stop mechanisms to prevent conflict.

Seeking Approval. Your child lacks adequate opportunities to feel accomplished and capable. She has little sense of her own self-worth because she has too few chances to see it actualized. If she is seeking approval from peer groups, she is not deriving enough power from her associations with you or the family. As a proactive parent, introduce increasingly challenging and fulfilling responsibilities that allow her to see the results of her achievement (i.e., gardening, cooking, art/design, journalism, and charity work) while building a sense of her own unique identity.

Because power equates so closely with identity in the teen years, the more her family power helps her build an identity, the less she will be compelled to seek approval from peers. What is unique about your family? What is your source of pride? What do you offer her that peers cannot?

Throughout this book you will find recommendations for proactive parenting. Some of the techniques suggested are simple, and some are more involved. Becoming proactive in your parenting takes time and practice, so do not pressure yourself. Stick with whatever disciplinary device you currently use until you feel ready to introduce new measures, always taking baby steps as you redefine your relationship with your child.

> Start small. The way to reinvent yourself as a parent is through gradual, progressive and authentic change.

Chapter Three
Responsibility

Responsibility is a healthy form of power for a child because it affirms self-worth while providing an avenue for the child to become an integral and contributing member of the family and community.

But responsibility has some negative connotations for both parents and children. It is the topic around which many battles ensue when parents, in an attempt to prepare their children for adulthood, give them responsibilities, often in the form of household chores. But the chores are often neglected or handled in a manner that the parent finds unsatisfactory, sparking a battle in which the parent assumes the role of nag and the child reacts with stubborn resentment.

To better understand this dynamic, let us look at an example. A common chore that parents delegate to their tweens or teens is yard work, such as mowing the yard, raking, pulling weeds, trimming hedges. The traditional approach is to define the child's tasks, his technique, and his work schedule, and then pass judgment on his performance. There might be an allowance or bonus to sweeten the deal, or the parent will simply smile approvingly when the job is done well or criticize when it is not.

Another approach is to have a discussion with the child about the yard and what it means to the family, and solicit his input about how it should look, its upkeep, and his vision for it in the short and long term.

What is the key difference between these two strategies? The first encourages the child to rely on the parent for direction and implies that the child's opinions and preferences have no value.

The second approach invites the child to think critically under the parent's wing and with the parent's leadership. With this approach to responsibility, the child is learning not only how to solve problems, but how to engender the respect and support of others in the process—skills that will serve him through life.

If your reaction to the second approach is "That would never happen," you may be surprised to know that I took that example from a real-life scenario in which the parents transformed their teenager from destructive and rebellious to constructive and engaged, all by soliciting his input and inviting him to take on challenges that were meaningful to the family as a whole.

So, as you consider the responsibility approach to parenting, keep in mind that there is a difference between responsibility that you impose on your child without offering him a voice in the matter and responsibility that your child owns. One is a form of servitude, and one is true empowerment and, of course, the child responds better to the latter.

EVERYDAY RESPONSIBILITY

Remember our list of everyday tasks from Chapter One? Now that we have had a closer look at the relationship between power and behavior, we can explore these tasks as ways to empower your child, promote his maturity and encourage a stronger parent-child bond.

You may still have reservations about offering your child responsibilities that you would rather continue doing because they bring you pleasure as a nurturer or because you are not yet comfortable allowing him to do them for himself. Stay within your comfort zone while looking for ways to move your child from a 1 to a 10 on the "power scale."

In order to start your child on a track of self-sufficiency, simply take some time to show him one of the tasks you are ready for him to do. Walk him through the steps for the task, covering as many details as possible. Let him show you what he has learned, and model again if you feel that you should.

COMMUNICATING BIG IDEAS TO LITTLE PEOPLE

To communicate with a **Wobbly Age** child, other parents recommend the use of images. Just about any idea can be communicated without words. Drawings, magazine tear-outs, picture books, movies and even your own theatrical role-plays can supplant or support communication with your little one. You will find strategies and parent-recommended resources for communicating with younger children in the Toolbox at the back of the book.

Be mindful of your approach, because there is a subtle, but significant, distinction between power that is given as a token and power that is structured to grow and deepen over time. For instance, letting your child decide what to eat for breakfast, with no modeling or context for making that decision, will likely yield unfavorable results. Inviting your child to assume gradual ownership of that process by showing him how tasks are done and how decisions are made in a system of ever-increasing responsibility will ensure his success and your satisfaction.

TEACHING RESPONSIBILITY THROUGH MODELING

You may recall from the Preface the way Ms. Yvonne modeled painting for her students. To model is to show, not tell. If you are a modeling parent, you spend very little time telling your child what to do. Instead, you introduce a skill, responsibility, or behavior through demonstration. This gives your child room to think and develop questions.

MODELING

Most of the everyday tasks listed in Chapter One can be taught rather easily to children of all ages. I have provided detailed guidance on modeling tasks like these on the next few pages.

SAMPLE TASK #1: WAKING UP

Walk through. Think through the process step by step. What is involved in setting the alarm clock? We take the tiny steps for granted, but when modeling, every detail counts.

Configure. What are the challenges for your child in doing this job? Does it require manual dexterity? Reading? Remembering? Timing? Think through the job, and configure it to accommodate your child's weaknesses. As a society, we often configure environments and tasks for the elderly or for those with special needs. We want those with physical limitations to feel powerful and self-sufficient. You want the same for your child.

For example, look at the alarm clock. If your child is of **Wobbly Age**, are the buttons distinguishable by color? Add color to them to help your child see the difference. Is the clock analog or digital? Analog works best for children, especially if the four quarters of the clock are marked by color (like four quarters of a pie chart). Look at the device, and think about how you can label it to make each important part stand out.

For children of **Lunchbox Age** or **Telephone Age**, include more discussion, partnering, strategizing and consensus-building in your modeling. Encourage your child to help you walk through, configure, and plan the complexity of the task.

Contextualize. With your child, model what to do, exactly as you want him to do it. If you want him to set the clock at bedtime, then model the behavior at bedtime. For **Wobbly Age** children, crawl into bed yourself to communicate the context of the step. In the morning, when the alarm sounds, model each step, from turning it off to moving on to the next task.

Tier. If possible, structure the task so that he first learns the simplest version and then builds upon what he knows. If you want him to change the time on the clock, add that step after he has demonstrated success with what you have taught him thus far.

SAMPLE TASK #2: EATING BREAKFAST

Another everyday task on our list is "preparing/eating breakfast." Follow the steps: walk through, configure, contextualize, and tier the job so that your child has a series of challenges to advance through.

Here are the minimum requirements for a child to prepare and eat breakfast independently, along with some questions to guide your modeling:

- Locating the cereal, bowl, spoon and milk.
  Are their locations labeled?
- Opening the cereal container and the milk container.
  Are the containers child-friendly and within reach?
- Pouring or scooping the cereal into a bowl; pouring the milk.
  Have you modeled technique and configured the containers for your child's ability?
- Eating.
  Have you modeled exactly where and how it's done?
- Disposing of food and either cleaning dishes or placing them somewhere to be cleaned.
  Is the garbage labeled and accessible? Did you model dish-cleaning?

SAMPLE TASK #3: BEDTIME

A third activity on our list was "recognizing a set bedtime." There is tremendous benefit to empowering your child with knowing when it is time to go to bed (on his own) and taking himself there. This is not to imply that you should not join him, read to him, or otherwise share in the bedtime process, but you do not have to poke and prod, beg and plead, or nag and threaten him to go to bed.

The "dance" so many parents do in putting their children to bed is unnecessary. If your child is empowered to handle bedtime on his own, and if he otherwise receives reliable attention from you, he will not feel compelled to use bedtime as a way to overpower you or capture your attention.

COACHING

We are familiar with the term "coaching" as it is used in other domains, such as sports. A coach in that context models technique and then provides pointers and encouragement as the athlete develops mastery.

In modeling, you demonstrate technique. In coaching, you pinpoint where strengthening is needed and help your child fine tune his method, either by providing additional modeling or by providing better tools.

For example, if you have a **Telephone Age** child, and you want him to learn how to manage time better, start with one aspect of his time management, such as his homework schedule. Together (because he is old enough to think through this with you), follow the four steps of modeling: walk through, configure, contextualize and tier.

Schedule time together each week or each month to talk about time management and offer tips and demonstrations to support his growth. As long as coaching is an explicit part of your plan, and you have tiered his responsibilities so that he has more challenges to look forward to, he will be receptive to your supportive, judgment-free guidance.

You are coaching when you invite your child to experiment with new skills, and then provide multiple opportunities for him to develop and improve those skills.

Coaching and modeling go hand in hand. Modeling gives your child technique, and coaching gives him support as he develops competency. Coaching is unconditional support for your child as he tries and as he fails, creating a safe haven for making mistakes and promoting independence and maturity.

In modeling his bedtime activity, begin where he would begin, be it the living room, the dining table, or the backyard. Walk yourself through each step, just as you would like him to do it. As you do this walk-through, you will become aware of the equipment he needs to do the task. If he needs to become aware of the time, then an alarm or clock should be available nearby or on his body (i.e., a wristwatch). If he needs to change into nightclothes, those should be stored within reach and labeled.

When you model a lengthy, multi-step process for him, model in segments, allowing him to copy you and demonstrate an understanding. Then, move on to the next step. You are in no hurry. If either of you becomes frustrated, table the task for tomorrow.

If you tier his responsibilities, then he will understand that timely and thorough completion of bedtime equates with moving up to more challenging (and therefore more appealing) responsibility. There is no failure for him. He simply remains at that level of responsibility until he demonstrates mastery.

SHARED RESPONSIBILITY

Have you considered sharing your own household responsibilities with your child? There is no better way to build your child's feeling of importance and inclusion in the family. Below I have provided steps for doing this.

You may need to adjust your thinking in order to consider your child a contributing member of the household, regardless of his age. Does your child have housekeeping responsibilities that are noticeable if they are ignored, like taking out the garbage or washing dishes? Is your child responsible for solving an important household problem, like organizing a storage closet so that things can be found? Does your child have leadership in the family, such as taking his turn at running a family meeting or preparing a plan for the household to become more environmentally friendly?

TIPS FOR AGE-APPROPRIATE RESPONSIBILITY

Wobbly Age: Children at this age will embrace any physical task as well as simple mental ones, like sorting.

Lunchbox Age: These children want intellectual challenges as well as physical tasks involving precision.

Telephone Age: Tweens and Teens want responsibilities that matter significantly to the family and involve planning, strategy, and decision-making.

Take care to avoid giving your child token jobs or titles; it is belittling for a child of any age to be given a task that has no impact on anyone and goes unnoticed if not done. Look beyond menial tasks for meaningful opportunities to enhance your child's development.

Also, when responsibility is shared with a child, there must be the expectation that the child, and only the child, will do the task. It will not work if someone comes behind her and does it correctly. Children recognize when that is occurring and will not take the responsibility seriously.

HOW TO SHARE RESPONSIBILITY WITH YOUR CHILD

Step 1: List Your Jobs. Reflect on your own responsibilities for the family and household. Jot down all of the duties that fall on your shoulders and the day-to-day tasks that you complete for yourself and others. This should include everything: grocery shopping, buying birthday cards, making home repairs, paying bills, and so on. Here are some items one parent listed:

My Responsibilities
Groceries
Bills
Walking the dog
Housecleaning
Watering plants

Add to this list any problems you experience in your day-to-day routine. Do you always lose your keys? Does the dog need to be walked more often? Do you sometimes find yourself short on ingredients for dinner? Is your family a scheduling nightmare? Are those photos piling up that you intended to put into albums? Think of this portion of the brainstorming as a "wish list" of assistance that can improve the day-to-day operations of the family.

Here are items the parent mentioned above added to her list. These are tasks that she felt would improve the running of her household or solve problems:

Smooth Operation Wish List
Get dinner prepared on time
File stacks of papers
Organize photos
Do laundry more regularly
Know when we are running out of...

Step 2: Consider Your Child's Abilities. With your list in hand, put a checkmark next to every item that *could*—with some training—be done or managed by your child. Open your mind and remember that children are motivated by the singular goal of becoming successful adults. If the job truly matters, your child will want it and will want to do it well. Of course, you will not check off tasks that put your child in danger, and you should choose only those tasks with which you are comfortable.

Rate each of the checked tasks according to your comfort level. If you have a spouse or partner, he or she, too, should make a list and rate tasks according to his/her comfort level. Then the two of you should compare notes and come to consensus.

The parent who created the lists above has a four-year-old. Here are the responsibilities from both lists that she felt comfortable sharing with her four-year-old. You will also see her rating system (1=most comfortable):

	My Responsibilities	
✓	Groceries (letting me know what we need using my checklist)	5
✓	Bills (opening them, organizing them, throwing away envelopes, etc.)	1
	Walking the dog	
✓	Housecleaning (dusting, dishes, mirrors, vacuuming, recycling)	3
✓	Watering plants (with labeled measuring cups)	2

Smooth Operation Wish List	
Get dinner prepared on time	
✓ File stacks of papers (separate into	7
stacks (bills, clippings, receipts, not sure)	
✓ Organize photos (by event? By person?)	6
Do laundry more regularly	
✓ Know when we are running out of...	4
(toilet paper, light bulbs,	

As you can see, this parent chose only the items that she felt comfortable sharing with her four-year-old. You may harbor some doubt about whether or not her four-year-old was capable of doing these tasks, but by following the next few steps, this parent achieved success. Let us look at how she structured the responsibilities she chose to share with her child.

Step 3: Create a Staircase. I call this the "staircase" approach because it begins with one easy step and little risk, and then each step builds on the one that came before it. As your child climbs this staircase, jobs become more critical, complex, and challenging; but with each step, your child is gaining competency and you are becoming more comfortable. The idea is to allow the child to start small, experience success, and gradually increase his level of responsibility from there.

Using your list and your comfort rating, create a staircase that your child can climb by performing responsibilities reliably and well. Give this process plenty of time and thought; it is critical to your success. Here is the staircase our sample parent created, based on her lists and comfort ratings:

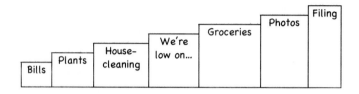

Step 4: Meet. Share your planning and your intentions with your child. Invite his reactions. Give him time to think about your proposal and to make suggestions of his own. Consider doing this as part of a family meeting.

Step 5: Model. Walk through, configure, contextualize and tier.

INNOVATIVE RESPONSIBILITIES

In the empowerment of your child, you are not limited to offering him a share only in standard household tasks. Below are some creative ideas from families who designed unique and engaging jobs for their children. As you will see, these jobs not only support the smooth functioning of your family, but enhance your lives and bring you closer.

GROCERY STOCKER (AGES 3+)

For busy parents, the job of making sure that the household is stocked with the groceries needed for everyday and special meals can be burdensome. Why not delegate this important job to your child?

This particular job may involve a regular (i.e., weekly) inventory of all groceries, or just key items. For example, you can restrict this job just to "pantry stock" (i.e., flour, spices, potatoes, cereals, canned goods, etc.), or you can make this a comprehensive responsibility that is tied to meal-planning.

If you are starting with a young child, take small steps by entrusting him with stocking 1-3 items, and then increase the scope of the responsibility as your child demonstrates success. Use images to represent items if your child is younger and cannot read.

As Grocery Stocker, your child can:

- Take inventory of food supplies
- Plan meals with a family member
- Create shopping lists
- Manage coupon clipping, organization, and use
- Supervise the grocery shopping trip
- Create a grocery shopping budget
- Manage a "grocery fund" with a set limit
- Alert a family member when supplies are low

HOUSE HOST (AGES 4+)

If you have friends or family coming for a visit, why not entrust their care and comfort to your child? Hardworking parents often cannot give proper thought to their guests, but children cherish the role of host.

As House Host, your child can:

- Clean the guestroom and change sheets
- Create a kind welcoming note or drawing
- Decorate the guestroom or house with flowers
- Supply guests with bathroom necessities

- Prepare refreshments to welcome guests
- Monitor the arrival of guests (i.e., flight arrival)
- Inquire about diet restrictions, allergies or other food issues
- Prepare a "tour" kit of suggested outings, brochures, Web sites, maps

GREEN GUARD (AGES 4+)

This responsibility involves monitoring your home's environmental impact and might include attention to energy and water usage or recycling.

As Green Guard, your child can:

- Conduct regular observations of the water and energy usage of family members using drawings, charts, computer tools, photographs or audio or video recordings
- Compile statistics and reports about the family's environmental behavior
- Research "green" methods of energy and water usage
- Design a recycling system for the family
- Conduct regular meetings with the family to discuss its green status

This is a wonderful opportunity to engage your child in real-world civic-minded action, not to mention an ideal vehicle for developing academic skills.

CALENDAR CAPTAIN (AGES 7+)

Most families of three or more people struggle with managing time and coordinating activities. With the proper tools and modeling, your child can become

Calendar Captain for your household and provide a welcome relief from the stress of scheduling in a busy family.

As Calendar Captain, your child can:

- Interview family members about their schedules
- Enter events and deadlines on the calendar
- Think through solutions when two activities conflict
- Plan and schedule activities for family togetherness

TRIP PLANNER (AGES 8+)

Too often, parents plan family trips without ever consulting or involving the children. It goes without saying that trip planning is a wonderful way to develop important academic and life skills, including geography, math, and organizational ability.

Entrusting your child with the job of planning, or leading the planning of your next family trip could begin with the decision about where to go, or the job could begin after that decision has been made. The earlier you involve your child, the better.

When making decisions about the trip, use consensus-building techniques with your spouse or partner and children. Consensus-building teaches your children how to make decisions by listening, problem-solving, working as a team, and making compromises for the benefit of the family as a whole.

> If you would like more guidance on holding effective family meetings and modeling consensus-building for your children, see the workbook companion to this book: *The Three P's of Parenting: A Family Workbook.*

As Trip Planner, your child can:

- Research "things to do" at the destination
- Interview the family about their preferences for activity, lodging, meals, etc.
- Conduct price comparisons for transportation, lodging, food and attractions
- Manage a "trip budget" with a set limit
- Present a proposal to the family on all aspects of the trip
- Communicate with travel agents and hotel staff
- Learn (and encourage the family to learn) a language associated with the trip
- Compile a packing list for each family member
- Prepare cameras and video cameras for the trip
- Design a route based on logic and family preferences

COMPUTER ENGINEER (AGES 10+)

It is a well-known fact that our children know more about computers than we do. So, why not charge your child with the responsibility of maintaining and, in some instances, troubleshooting computer problems experienced by family members?

You need not be computer literate in order to empower your child to do this. Your child simply needs resources and then modeling of how to use those resources.

Take a trip to the library or bookstore, and help your child find software or computer manuals that support the kind of technical responsibilities he will have. Consider hiring a computer expert for an hour or two to coach your child in the necessary skills. Sometimes, even the school's technology expert can be of help.

If you have two children some years apart, the older child can be entrusted with the responsibility of protecting the younger by keeping the Internet "child-friendly" and working to protect his sibling from online predators or inappropriate material. You will be amazed at the shift in attitude your teen adopts regarding "Internet integrity" once charged with the protection of a younger sibling.

As Computer Engineer, your child can:

- Optimize computer performance
- Install new software
- Secure the internet for younger children
- Create and manage computer files
- Store digital family photos and video
- Introduce the family to new technology
- Upgrade computer systems as needed

How to Teach Your Child Responsibility

1. BRAINSTORM together the important aspects of the job. What actions does it require? What would be the best approach? Look at examples.

2. GENERATE A LIST of actions that comprise the job. Be as detailed or as general as you like. For younger children, use images to represent words and ideas.

3. ROLE-PLAY any actions that require interpersonal skill.

4. DEMONSTRATE (model) any actions that require manual skill.

5. WELCOME MISTAKES as part of learning.

6. COACH your child along the way, showing trust, allegiance and encouragement.

Options for engaging your child as a contributing member of the family are limitless. Include your child in your planning, and he will delight in coming up with ways to volunteer his services as your partner and assistant.

TROUBLESHOOTING

You may experience some glitches as you try to increase your child's level of responsibility. Here is what might happen and what to do if it does:

The tasks seem too risky for my child's age. Remember that you can adjust responsibilities to suit your comfort level. If something important is at risk, and you cannot afford to have mistakes, simply modify the responsibility to exclude those things that worry you, and put risky tasks higher on your child's "responsibility staircase."

My child is not doing his job. If your child neglects or refuses to carry out a responsibility that he has agreed to, his behavior is most likely tied to one of these explanations:

- He feels he has no choice.

If you think he feels trapped in this job, then he may not have had enough voice in the initial choice. Revisit his options, being sure that he has a tier of ever more sophisticated jobs on the horizon. Does he understand that he will advance with each success?

- He feels incompetent and embarrassed.

It is possible that the job he has taken on has not been

modeled in enough detail, or enough times. Introduce more specific guidance into your modeling of this job. Provide pictures, charts, or better labeling of the tools he is using. Check your reactions to his attempts to be sure that you are not being overly critical or judgmental.

- He is seeking attention.

If he is getting more attention from you as a result of not doing his jobs, then he may be seeking that attention. The next chapter provides more insight and guidance on your child's attention-seeking behavior.

I feel compelled to fix my child's mistakes. When you decide to entrust your child with new responsibility, you may be tempted to come behind him to fix his mistakes. However, doing so sends a message to him that you do not believe that he is capable.

First, ask yourself if this job is within your comfort zone for allowing mistakes. Naturally, if mistakes create serious problems for you or the family, then elevate this job so that he must prove himself in less critical jobs first.

However, if you feel the job is appropriate for your child, but you want to decrease his chances of making mistakes, try:

- re-modeling the skills in more detail or with more regularity;
- having regular review sessions in which you invite your child to ask questions; or
- photographing or videotaping the job as you model it, so that he can review it privately.

Meaningful Responsibility: A Case Study in Pet Ownership

Before we close this chapter, and this segment on power, let us look at a responsibility that has deep and lasting empowerment for your child: pet ownership. This is a job suitable for any child age 3 or older and is one that many parents seem eager to introduce, although it seldom materializes as they would hope.

In the discussion of pet ownership, I am not referring to situations in which the parent wants a pet, brings one home and then invites the child to participate in its care. That is Shared Responsibility, which we covered earlier in the chapter. Here, I am referring to a situation in which the parent buys or adopts a pet for the sole purpose of entrusting it to the child's care.

Pet ownership differs from many of the responsibilities we have covered in this chapter because it is a lifetime commitment (for the life of the pet), and because failure to properly care for the pet carries dire consequences. That is why most parents entrusting pet care to their children for the first time eventually assume that responsibility themselves.

Entrusting your child with a serious responsibility and then taking that job away has a potentially lasting negative effect on your child. For this reason, launching pet ownership should involve considerable thought and discussion beforehand.

With that stated, if you have had negative experiences with pet ownership in the past, I hope that this example offers inspiration to try again; owning a pet can be a catalytic growth experience for your child.

Life Lessons from a Goldfish

A third grader came home from school after hearing about his friend's new goldfish, and convinced his mother to buy him one. Later that week, they spotted a pet store, went in, and left with a small goldfish in a plastic bag filled with water.

Choosing the Pet

The best way to select a pet for your child is to first determine which pets you feel comfortable entrusting to his care and the heartiness of the pet should it receive substandard care. If there is no pet you are comfortable taking this risk with, consider starting your child with a plant, with the understanding that he must prove that he can care for it before getting a pet.

At the pet store that day, the child's mother picked up a book on goldfish care, as she knew very little about fish of any kind. The book was written for adults, so when she urged her son to read it, he made meager attempts but soon gave up.

Mom filled the bowl with water, placed the rocks and plastic greenery in it, and plopped the fish in. Her son stared with fascination for nearly an hour, and then went about doing other things.

For several days, the son was diligent in the care of his fish. Mom had explained how to sprinkle the food, and so he did so, often. Perhaps too often. The water became cloudy quickly, and after a week, Mom had changed the water several times, becoming increasingly frustrated at the nuisance such a small creature was causing.

> ### COMMITMENT IS IN THE PREPARATION
>
> Ideally, you and your child will spend time studying the desired pet before bringing it home. Visit a bookstore or library, use the Internet, or talk to pet shop owners. The more effort your child puts forth in preparing for the pet, the more intrinsic his ownership of it will be. Encourage him to take what he learns and use it to prepare the ideal habitat for the pet before the pet is brought home, just as you may have prepared before bringing him home as a baby.

In her quick read of the goldfish manual, the mother had not realized how frequently the water would need to be changed when using a bowl. She was now beginning to realize that a tank would soon be necessary to avoid poisoning the fish. Just the thought of the expense and maintenance of a tank made her begin to regret ever consenting to the fish in the first place.

> ### MODELING BUILDS UNDERSTANDING
>
> You can better ensure your child's success with a responsibility if you show him all of the steps involved. Use the modeling techniques described earlier in this book: walk through the steps of the job, configure the job for your child's age, contextualize when and where the job is to be done, and tier the task so that he assumes ever-increasing responsibility.

A month after they brought the goldfish home, the son walked in to find it floating on the surface. He ran to tell his mother. He was anxious. His mother was distraught. She told him that they would have to flush the fish down the toilet. New to the experience of death, her son had a flood of questions like, "Why is he upside down?" His mother, herself upset, feeling guilty, angry and frustrated, had no clear answers.

> **RESPONSIBILITY FOR LIFE**
>
> If you truly entrust the pet's care to your child, then you are taking a risk that it may suffer from his neglect or mistakes. If you intervene to save the pet by taking over its care, you will send a message to your child that he is not capable of handling the task. Instead, choose a pet (with him) that requires minimal care, and model proper care for him along the way. If your child experiences loss of the pet, regardless of the cause, it is important that he have another opportunity to build on what he has learned and experience success.

If your child fails at or abandons his responsibility, you have not lost the valuable teaching and nurturing moments that were invested in him. A rich opportunity is created by failure—that of evaluating choices, finding solutions, and making amends. The same techniques that were used to launch the endeavor can be used to reevaluate it.

When you approach your child's responsibilities as practice fields for learning new and increasingly complex skills, you will instinctively know the right response when he falters.

POWER, PROTECTION AND RESPONSIBILITY

Responsibility is an efficient tool for parenting. Why? Because it addresses power *and* protection, two of the three P's, in one stroke. We have talked about how responsibility offers power to your child, but how does it offer him protection?

When you introduce your child to new skills, modeling, explaining, and nurturing him towards proficiency, you are preparing him for life. Through your coaching and through the execution and practice of responsibilities, he is learning how to make decisions, weigh pros and cons, research, organize, budget, and meet expectations. In addition, he is learning how to care for and be accountable to others.

In essence, you are outfitting him for the challenges that lie ahead and for successfully navigating and building relationships. There is no better form of protection than properly equipping your child for what is to come.

Now, let us look at the idea of protection in more depth so that you will recognize when your child is signaling you about this need and know how to respond.

Part Two

Protection

Chapter Four
Protection and Attention

For children, attention equates with protection. They cannot defend themselves, and they are largely dependent on others; so, instinctively, they look for confirmation that parents are not only watching them, but watching over them. When your child knows that you see her, she is comforted and reassured of her security. When she is not sure that she has your attention, or when she cannot predict when she will have it, her world feels less certain, and she is likely to seek reassurance.

In this chapter, I will reveal the various ways that your child uses attention-getting behaviors to satisfy her need for protection, and how you can use preventive measures to reassure her and promote a healthier parent-child dynamic.

THE ANGER-PROTECTION CYCLE

It may surprise you to learn that your child sometimes *seeks* your angry attention, but pause for a moment and think about how you look when you are angry. Your body becomes more imposing and your posture more erect. Your voice is more commanding, and you generally exhibit the characteristics of someone who can win a fight.

An angry parent exhibits power and strength— qualities that reassure a child that she is protected. Naturally, she would rather see her protector strong than defeated. Your anger may instill your child with fear, anguish, guilt, or even resentment; but a child who lacks protection will seek anger anyway, because angry attention is better than none.

THE TEST OF LEADERSHIP

Your child is especially prone to provoking your anger when she senses that you are weak, because your weakness makes her doubt your ability to protect. I call this the Test of Leadership. If you are feeling out of sorts, confused about an important decision, anxious, depressed, exhausted from work, or in some state of instability—these are the occasions when your child is likely to behave in a way that angers you.

If you are a single parent, or your relationship with your partner or spouse is experiencing more dissonance than usual, especially if divorce or separation is looming or underway, then your child may be acting out to anger you and find reassurance that you are strong and capable. This reaction to your fragility is not a conscious behavior, but your child's instinctive survival response.

Your child may also resort to The Test of Leadership

in school-related situations. You may be surprised to learn that many parent-teacher conferences are actually products of your child's attempts to test your leadership. Let us look at this dynamic more closely.

A teacher will call a parent-teacher conference if your child is misbehaving regularly or performing poorly in school. But what was the real force leading up to the need for this conference? The answer is in how this situation makes you behave, and what your child gains from it.

When you receive the news from the teacher, you are likely to be shocked, concerned and perhaps even angry. You might even be embarrassed, because you likely did not know that there was a problem. So, your child may receive angry and concerned attention from you, and most likely it is *undivided* attention.

At the conference, the child is either present while you face the teacher, or nearby waiting for the outcome. Either way, while the child certainly experiences fear and apprehension, she also experiences protection. You are there not only to find out what trouble she has caused, but, in her mind, you are there to defend her, represent her, and buffer her from the teacher's angst. On a subconscious level, your child is satisfying her need for feeling protected by behaving in a way that compels the teacher to summon you.

It is no coincidence that the teacher who requests a conference with you is usually one that your child does not like or finds intimidating. In those instances, you have been "brought" there by your child to present a powerful force that can stand up to that teacher.

So, if you feel awkward at a parent-teacher conference, in the dark about the problem and confused about whether to defend your child or side with her teacher, you now understand why you are there. It is not to address an academic issue, but to satisfy your child's need to feel protected, either with your anger or your defense.

The true solution to the problem is to use proactive measures to address the need (for protection) that led your child to bring you there.

How To Prevent The Anger-Attention Cycle

The cycle of behavior and reaction that you may be experiencing with your child can be broken by changing just one of its elements. Here are some suggestions for breaking that cycle:

Relaxation Discipline. Your child moves you to anger because she believes this is how to invoke your strength. By puffing up, you affirm her belief. To de-program her behavior, alter your reaction to show her that making you angry will not yield the desired result. At the same time, introduce behavior that builds your parent-child bond. This relaxation strategy works especially well with young children.

What both of you need in a moment of tension is to dispel stress. If possible, remove yourselves from public view; otherwise, move to a corner or less populated space. Squat to get eye level with your child, but do not insist on eye-to-eye contact. Use your body position to get close enough to her so that she can hear you whisper, but maintain a small degree of physical space for both of you.

If, at this point, all you do is maintain this position quietly for a minute or two, you will already have begun to de-program your child's anger-seeking behavior and reduce your own stress. If you are interested in building more from this experience, try the following:

Start breathing, using the technique of inhaling through your nose and filling your stomach (not your chest), and then releasing by blowing through your mouth. I call this the "birthday breath," because I teach children to do it by explaining that they are smelling a birthday cake and then blowing out the candles, imagining the cake's smell and flavor as they inhale, imagining the glowing candles as they exhale. I encourage you to teach your child to use this breathing technique whenever she experiences stress.

As you introduce breathing, channel your energy into a low voice (low = strong), and repeat a phrase that calms you both such as "relax" or "breathe" or "it's ok." The mistake that many parents make in a moment of anger is to try to talk through the experience. Children rely mostly on your body language; there is no need to talk when you are recovering from anger. Simply breathe, position your body to show control, and allow the feelings to subside. The less you say the better.

If your child is accustomed to provoking your anger, this new approach will confuse her. She may attempt to move away from you or otherwise resist your efforts to soothe the situation. Keep your goals small and achievable: thirty seconds of stillness on the first attempt; a full minute on the second; and so on. Focus on limiting or avoiding an angry reaction, distancing yourself emotionally, and removing stress from the situation. Do not be disappointed if you are unsuccessful on the first try. It took your child many attempts to program you; it will take you at least a few to *de*-program her.

Later, once you and your child have had some time to relax, compose your thoughts and establish some emotional distance from the stressful experience, consider using one or more of the following techniques to address what initially caused the behavior.

Role-Play. In the heat of a moment of anger with a child, most parents find it challenging to stop and become conscious of what is happening. Role-play can help you prepare for those moments and break the cycle of behavior that intensifies them.

A WORD ABOUT ROLE-PLAY

For our purposes, role-play is a process of acting out experiences so that you can look at those experiences more closely and understand the dynamic that makes them happen as they do. Role-play is one of my favorite parenting strategies, because it can be done with younger and older children, is simple and engaging, can be used to address every parenting problem, and promotes bonding. Therefore, you will see it suggested periodically throughout this book.

Because role-play is not a commonly used family tool, you are likely to feel somewhat strange upon introducing it to your child and other family members. Just remember that your parenting is only as visionary as the tools you are willing to bring to it. You will reap endless rewards from making this technique an integral part of your approach.

Invite someone you trust, such as your spouse or partner, a close friend, or an extended family member, to help you reenact the incidents in which you are most likely to lose your temper with your child. Take turns with your partner, switching roles, so that you can develop a more objective understanding of the dynamic that happens when you become angry.

Give some thought to the patterns of your anger. When does it happen? Where? Which of your child's behaviors are most likely to make you upset? By spotting those contextual cues in a role-play, you will be more conscious of them when they occur in real life.

Think through your reactions to your child's behavior. Practice an alternative approach, or invent words or phrases that serve as "peace codes" between you and your child (hint: employ your child's help with this).

If you have a **Lunchbox Age** child or a **Telephone Age** child, consider including her in the role-play. "What?!"

you ask. "Include my own child in a role-play about my anger?" Yes, naturally. Children are masters of role-play, and by dissecting with her a problem that involves you both, you are likely to get helpful feedback and insights.

Together, pick which incident you want to reenact. Invite her to choose which role she would like to portray. Ask her to direct the action, telling you what to do and say. You will be surprised at how much you learn about her and about yourself. Children of all ages love role-play and will usually share thoughts and feelings in it that they do not express otherwise, because it is a non-threatening form of communication.

The beauty of role-playing each other is that in the process of defining the problem, the incidents, the behaviors and the reactions, you will, in essence, address them. But you will do so in a safe, engaging, and often entertaining way. You will giggle and debate and grow closer in the process.

Demonstrate Strength. If your child is provoking your anger with some frequency, you may appear weak or uncertain to her. She may sense a void of leadership. You can comfort her doubts by giving her more opportunities to see your strength and confidence. Does she see you when you are at your best? Are your shining moments hidden from her because they all take place at work or outside the home?

Reflect on your personal strengths and make more opportunities for her to witness them. Where possible, offer her a glimpse of you in postures of success, determination, decision-making, problem-solving and especially protection of others. She only needs to witness you in your glory occasionally; she will log that information and refer to it for a long time to come.

Share Leadership. In Chapter Three, we reviewed numerous ways to empower your child with responsibility. If you are experiencing a personal defeat, a professional decline, or a feeling that the weight of the world is upon you, now is the time to employ responsibility as a mechanism for bringing your child closer. Parental instinct may tell you to hide your feelings from your child in times of weakness, but that is an ideal time to bring your child into your process of leadership and invite her partnership.

First, you cannot hide your weaknesses from your child; she watches you too closely and too constantly for you to shield her from your foibles. If you attempt to hide your problems from her, she will sense that something is wrong and may even internalize blame for it.

Second, by not inviting her help, you send her a conflicting message: "I am weak, and you cannot support me." In doing this, you render her, in her view, both vulnerable and powerless. She will then be compelled to stimulate your fiercer side, or to seek leadership and protection from someone else.

So in times of trial and tribulation, remember that your child can be your most valuable ally. By allowing her partnership, you empower her and reduce her anger-seeking behaviors.

RELIABLE ATTENTION

Your child wants your undivided attention, but in a manner that she can predict. Spurts of your time or efforts to compensate for inattention with large chunks of togetherness are cold comfort for her because what she wants is to know that she can rely on your attention and will not have to share it.

If you are a stay-at-home parent, you may have no difficulty giving your child undivided attention. The struggle may be in finding time and space to attend to yourself. Both situations—parents having little time to give and having little time for themselves—are addressed in this section.

If you have an erratic schedule of time with your child or make commitments to your child that you do not keep, she will likely use attention-seeking behaviors such as those outlined below:

The Pleaser. One technique that attention-seeking children often use is to please you beyond your wildest expectations. However, we tend to give less attention to well-behaved children than to those who are misbehaving; so to succeed with the pleasing approach, a child will strive to overachieve (usually in school or extracurricular activities) or become indispensable to you as a helper.

A child who is overachieving to keep your attention is never satisfied with her performance and campaigns constantly to convince you that she can do more or do it better. She has your attention as long as you believe she can do better; but once she satisfies you, she has to raise the bar still higher.

The one who seeks to become indispensable to you believes your reliance on her secures your attention. She will spot any task that burdens you and take it on, even competing with adults in the house to outshine them and secure your attention and devotion away from them.

The Menace. Another technique a child will use to get reliable attention from you is to resort to extreme behaviors that elicit your fear or anger. She will start with small transgressions or brushes with danger and then intensify them until she gets a reaction from you.

If she succeeds in gaining your attention, only to lose it again, she will continue to escalate her behavior until capturing your attention again.

The Tease. Another way children deal with unreliable attention is to reject you altogether. The child will retreat from you to avoid feeling rejected when you are not available. When you notice the withdrawal and seek her out, a "cat and mouse" game ensues. The child learns that retreating is an effective way to get your attention.

Children often experience unreliable attention upon the birth of a new sibling, or when the parent takes on a new job or spouse/partner. What typically follows are alternating droughts and floods of attention, as well as broken promises as parents try to compensate for the lack of attention by making commitments they cannot keep.

The child who receives unpredictable attention is like a salesperson working on commission. Because she cannot predict when and where the next "paycheck" of attention will come, she cannot afford to relax and expect attention to be there when she needs it. Instead, she is constantly working to secure more, and more is never enough.

How To Provide Reliable Attention

Small Commitments. Busy parents worry about the amount of time they spend with their children. Quantity is far less important than reliability when it comes to time commitments. Start with 15 minutes a day, or even 15 minutes a week. If, for example, you cannot do storytime every night, then choose three nights of the week, and commit to those. Or, agree to three nights of the week, and meet with your child at the beginning of each week, when you have a better sense of your schedule, to choose which nights will be storytime nights.

UNDIVIDED ATTENTION

Note that undivided attention must be truly undivided. Time spent alone in the same room with you while you are working does not satisfy your child's need for attention. A child feels certain of your protection only when you are engaging her in some fashion: with eye contact, physical contact or conversation.

Put your child's name on your calendar. Keep your shared time sacred; let nothing interfere. Show your child her name in your planner, and observe her pride in knowing that time with her is as important as your high-level business meetings. Remember, too, that it is the imperviousness of the time that she values more than its length.

While there is no substitute for spending time with you, your child will also respond to having reliable attention from you by telephone, letters, email, and even instant messaging, if you are traveling or live in a separate household. Just remember not to commit to any of these options unless you can deliver.

You will be amazed at the impact that just a few minutes of reliable attention can have on your child. Of course, you must prove your reliability, so do not expect immediate results until after you have kept your commitments a few times. But once you exhibit a pattern of delivering on your commitments, your child will become increasingly calm and comfortable with the attention you are providing, and you should see a decline in her attention-seeking behaviors.

Look for pockets of time that you can spend with your child on a predictable basis. For instance, you might schedule a 15-minute walk with your child after the family dinner, a 15-minute phone call at bedtime when you are traveling, a 15-minute ride to pick up pastries on Sunday morning, a 15-minute shared bathroom time before work every morning. There are pockets in everyone's day, and a pocket or two of reliable time goes a long way in comforting your child's needs.

Integrated Time Commitments. One technique for enhancing the amount of time spent with your child is to attach that time to another need you have. For example, if you need to build more exercise into your routine, why not make your exercise time a shared experience with your **Wobbly Age** child? If you enjoy charitable, environmental, or community-building activities, partner with your **Lunchbox Age** child in your volunteer time. If you have been meaning to make changes to the house, such as closing in the garage for added space, why not develop that into a long-term project that includes your **Telephone Age** child, with the two of you working side by side.

SHOULD YOU INCLUDE THE FAMILY?

If you choose to bring your child into your personal activities, ensure that you do so in a way that keeps you engaged with her throughout the activity, and do not include others, especially siblings. Only include a partner or spouse if the two of you both direct your attention to the child, and not to each other. Create other opportunities for whole-family sharing, and reserve these occasions to focus solely on your child.

Another technique for making time commitments to your child is to take an otherwise onerous task, like bill-paying, and turn it into a life lesson for your child. Why not teach your child how you pay bills, as you do it? Teach her how you do your weekly housekeeping, how to weed the garden, or how to organize the garage, as you do it. As long as you have the patience to extend the time it takes for that task so that you can genuinely teach your child, you satisfy two needs, yours and hers, at once.

"Me" Time. Both work-away and stay-at-home parents struggle with finding "me" time; both need that time for sanity and for getting things done that require focus or privacy.

The biggest challenge in defining "me" time is in helping your child understand when that time is in effect, and when it is over. Your child will respect those boundaries if 1) communication is clear, 2) the timing is consistent and reliable, and 3) she can anticipate having your undivided attention at some point.

If you are a stay-at-home parent, you may believe that being home all day makes it unnecessary for you to worry about scheduling time with your child. On the contrary, you have the more difficult challenge of helping your child understand when it is her time, and when it is not. Doing this is critical, not just because it is healthy for you to have personal time, but because she needs to have a reliable expectation for your undivided attention and the ability to be independent of you and respect your boundaries when it is not her time with you. You are, of course, also modeling the setting of boundaries, which is a life skill that she will use throughout the course of her life.

Introduce "me" time into your weeks by designating one or more evenings and specific timeframes during which you and your child each do your own activities under the same roof. Support your child's ability to work or play without you by helping her create a list of "me" time activities, and be sure to model those that are new to her.

"Me" time activities that your child can do while at home with you might include: journaling, drawing, painting, watching TV, exercising, practicing an instrument, gardening, pen pal letter writing, building with blocks, calling relatives to chat (yes, children can do this on their own with the right setup), teaching the dog new tricks, working in a learning center (more on this later), IM-ing with friends, homework, etc.

If your child can anticipate that, for example, Tuesday night is a "me" night and Wednesday is an "us" night, she will be more relaxed about spending time without your undivided attention. If, however, she cannot predict when she will have you to herself, she may seek you out constantly.

Many parents alter their lives dramatically when a child is born, feeling that self-sacrifice is fundamental to the parent's role. Those parents will sometimes give up too much of what they care about in order to fulfill what they believe is their duty to their child. Over time, they grow resentful toward the child for the sacrifices they were "forced" to make.

Children are meant to adapt to us, and they want to adapt to us. If you are a freelance worker with unpredictable hours, you do not have to change jobs in order to be a good parent. What you can and should do, however, is create systems through which your child can accurately predict when she will have your attention. Giving your child an absolutely reliable 15 minutes a week is better than leaving her to guess about her next opportunity to see you.

If you have an occupation that involves unannounced travel or responding to emergencies, it is perfectly reasonable to expect your child to understand your sudden absences. Circumstances like these are part of a family's culture, and the child should be expected to adapt to that culture. In extreme cases, introduce simple commitments of attention (even via phone or instant messaging) into the moments you know that you can control.

If you have a spouse or partner (or ex-spouse/partner) with whom you are able to work constructively, talk together about your commitments to your child before you make them. You want your spouse/partner to be confident and supportive of your decisions when you are not present so that your child receives one solid reassuring message that you are trustworthy.

Attention to Siblings. Most parents of siblings would agree that their children have unique behaviors. There is usually an over-achiever and an under-achiever. In families of three or more children, there is also usually a "baby" of the family.

If you think about this pattern, it makes sense. If they behaved alike, siblings would be "splitting the vote" of your attention. By choosing distinct behaviors, they are attempting to monopolize your attention. If one is demanding your praise for good deeds while the other is needing correction for mischief, you must choose, but cannot easily attend to both at once.

For families with three or more children, the situation is more complex. The third will usually choose to hold onto infantile behaviors as long as possible because the first and second children have captured the market on achievement and rebellion. Infantile behavior is quite effective, because it provokes a deep-seated protective instinct in the parent, and thus it can usually win attention away from other, older siblings.

Once a fourth child enters the picture, however, the rules of the game change. At that point, the parent has precious little time to spare, so the youngest (and neediest) is automatically going to receive the most attention. The second youngest will then seek attention from one of the older children. If the family continues to grow, the oldest siblings are likely to assume the roles of surrogate parents, and the cycle of attention-seeking will begin to revolve around them more than the parents themselves.

Strategic intervention and proactive parenting are the cures for the niche behaviors that children adopt in an effort to get your attention. If you have more than one child, and they are developing identities such as those of rebels, infants or over-achievers, they are competing with one another using patterns of behavior that will attract your attention. To eliminate this problem and free each of them to build unique identities that are constructive and mature, use the suggestions mentioned earlier for small and integrated commitments to satisfy your children's needs, but add elements of balance and fairness to ensure that each sibling receives attention of equal value and reliability.

Consider offering a variety of opportunities for your children to spend one-on-one time with you (e.g., going grocery shopping, visiting the batting cages, morning swim, pizza night, etc.), and periodically rotate your children through those experiences so that each child has fair and balanced access to you.

In this chapter, we have looked at how children use behavior to draw your attention and ensure that you are providing adequate, reliable protection. However, there are areas of your child's life in which your protection is needed, but she may not know how to alert you. In these cases, you may not be able to rely on your child's behavior signals as clues for where to direct your attention. Therefore, let us explore these "overlooked zones" so that you know where they are and can address your child's needs accordingly.

Chapter Five
Overlooked Protection

You are the knight-in-shining-armor for your child. He looks to you to defend him, rescue him, and accompany him in the face of a threat. Your allegiance to him in the presence of others makes him feel confident and secure.

When you insist that both his peers and superiors respect his physical, emotional, and intellectual space, you model for him an invaluable lesson in self-respect and personal boundaries that prepares him for all future relationships. In defending him, you show him that, while others can disagree with or reject him, no one has the right to attack him; and you teach him how to handle it when they do.

Allegiance to our children, however, is a component of protection that is often overlooked or misinterpreted. The modern parent gives significant attention to *correcting* the child, but too little to preparing him for real-world experiences and shaping a parent-child alliance that the child knows he can turn to in times of trouble.

A child who is constantly corrected grows to see his parents as "judge and jury" and will perform for their approval. A child who is protected through coaching, preparation and a sense of his parents' allegiance grows to see his parents as something akin to a fierce and capable legal team. He will trust and confide in them.

Taking the example of grades, a child who feels that his parents judge his academic performance is likely to conceal poor grades from them. A child who views his parents as guides with ideas and strategies for overcoming academic problems will seek them out for help.

Because even the most well-intentioned parents can overlook the importance of allegiance to their children, let us examine the zones in which children often feel under-protected, including:

- self-worth
- aggression at school
- sibling relationships
- predators
- imaginary threats (for young children)

Zone #1: Self-Worth

Children are often undermined in the area of their self-worth, particularly by their peers and occasionally by adults. For example, it is a violation of self-worth when a child is laughed at or is called "stupid" when he makes mistakes. It is also an attack on self-worth when he is mocked by a group of children (bullies) because of physical appearance, race, religion, gender, or any other aspect of his persona.

Some dismiss these types of behaviors as natural, arguing that in the "real world" kids must learn to stick up for themselves. However, there is nothing in our natural makeup that predisposes us to mock or disdain others; nor are we naturally equipped to know how to respond constructively to such attacks. Personal attacks are learned behaviors and are practiced and proliferated in settings where supervising adults are not properly trained to manage them. Your child needs protection in these circumstances, but may not know how to seek it.

In other instances, a teacher or other professional may violate your child's self-worth by suggesting that he is incapable of achieving a goal or is lacking moral fiber. Teachers can fall victim to labeling children as lazy, dishonest, or unruly. A child who is exposed to a teacher's prejudice for a sustained period of time may find himself conforming to the teacher's label, activating a self-fulfilling prophecy of behavior. Again, your child needs protection in these circumstances but may not know how to seek it.

How To Protect Self-Worth

Role-Play. In preparing your child to interact with others, use role-play to give him an opportunity to practice what to do and say. Avoid teaching him defensive behavior because this is what the child who is attacking him is seeking. Children who insult other children are deeply insecure; they want to feel powerful (because they are not), and they want attention (because they do not get enough).

Instead of teaching your child to be defensive, consider using this as an opportunity to teach him skills of diplomacy, political strategy and persuasion. Consider coaching him in how to read the behavior of his attackers and devise responses that go right to the heart of their motivations.

USING ROLE-PLAY TO PREEMPT CONFLICT

Acting out potential scenarios provides children a laboratory in which to experiment with their reactions to sensitive or potentially dangerous encounters. You can use role-play to prepare your child for emotional or physical attacks, or for negotiating unfamiliar dangers such as "hot stoves" for toddlers or "drugs at parties" for teens.

Here are some tips for getting the most from this approach:

- Assume any role your child wants you to play, and switch so that your child can experience different perspectives.

- Start gently, and gradually intensify the challenge as your child is ready to face it. Giggles are fine at first; but after that initial shyness subsides, encourage a serious, focused participation. If your child is not responsive, then try again another day.

- With **Wobbly Age** or **Lunchbox Age** children, use puppets, dolls, stuffed animals, action figures or any representative object to give your child the distance he needs to explore situations. It is easier for children to express fear and anger, and they are more likely to reveal the behaviors of bullies and predators if they can project those feelings and behaviors onto objects or characters in stories.

- Picture books and movies with related scenarios can provide context for your role-play. Consider shopping for these first and initiating role-play after viewing and discussing the story lines.

See the Toolbox in the back of the book for a list of resources and steps to help with your role-play.

For example, since most attacks occur in front of an audience of peers, does your child know how to address the crowd rather than the attacker? Does he know how to spin an argument while maintaining his self-respect? Does he know how to defuse an attack by giving an unexpected response? If the attack is by a teacher or another adult, does the child know how to respond subtly, to avoid appearing disrespectful?

If you feel ill-equipped to give him this type of guidance, visit the bookstore or library with him, or go online, and look together for guides on this topic. If you have a **Wobbly Age** or **Lunchbox Age** child, why not make books like *King of the Playground* or *How to Be Cool in the Third Grade* part of your nightly storytime experience? If your child is of **Telephone Age**, pick up a copy of *How to Win Friends and Influence People for Teen Girls* (written by Dale Carnegie's daughter!) or *Difficult People: Dealing with Almost Anyone* by Jennifer Rozines Roy (see the Toolbox in the back of the book for more suggestions).

Remember that the greatest value of role-play is that your child experiences confrontation with *you* first, rather than receiving an unexpected emotional jolt from a stranger. *What* he is prepared to do in reaction to an attack is not as important as knowing that one will come and how to recognize it.

Creed and Coat of Arms. Having a clear system of beliefs provides your child with certainty and armored self-esteem when confronted with attacks on his self-worth. What is your family's creed? Your source of pride? If you feel uncertain of the answers, spend time developing a family creed together with your child (if he is old enough). Talk about what makes you proud, your points of strength, factors that distinguish you from other families, and what you value most in life.

While the tradition of having a coat of arms is long-outdated, there is power in having a visual representation of your family's creed. Consider enlisting the help of your child to create images and symbols that make up this coat of arms. You might be surprised to see how this simple activity and the beliefs it confirms serve to bolster your child in the face of a personal attack. Sometimes, just knowing and believing in themselves is all children need in order to deal gracefully with adversity.

ZONE #2: AGGRESSION AT SCHOOL

Children need coaching in how to establish and defend their physical boundaries against aggression by their peers at school. Unfortunately, teachers and other child-related professionals are not always trained to manage incidents of aggression. Even the best teacher education programs focus primarily on delivery of curriculum content, with only a small portion of teacher training dedicated to the management of child behavior in a group setting. You are the best source of protection your child has against attacks that occur at school.

Recess is where most of these physical attacks occur against children. Nonetheless, a number of adults defend recess as an important part of a child's day. During recess, teachers are not as watchful of child behavior as they are in the classroom, partly because they need a break and partly to give children the freedom of unstructured playtime.

However, if you observe closely, you will see that recess is an acutely primal experience that offers little in the way of freedom, while reinforcing a social order defined largely by children. Most recess behaviors resemble those of our earliest ancestors. Children with strong alpha tendencies take control of those who are weaker. Children with deep insecurities either attack as bullies or find themselves tyrannized by one.

The most popular games during recess are based on hunting (i.e., hide-and-seek) or tribalism (i.e., Red Rover). Those who seek peaceful activities are often disrupted by those who seek dominance; and even peaceful activities, like jumping rope, hoola hoops and clapping games, typically involve the purposeful and often hurtful exclusion of others.

Perhaps worst of all, children can find themselves the target of innocent but nonetheless invasive violations. A girl at recess may find herself pursued and cornered by a band of boys compelled by their own primal group dynamic to aggress her with subtle sexual violations, like looking under her clothes, kissing her or touching her sexually. Boys have also been known to be subjected to similar group aggression by girls, including taunting and ridicule.

These groups are often led by an alpha child who is proving power by leading others in daring acts. The giggles and titters of the followers spur the leader on to try even more scandalous behaviors. In middle and high school, these behaviors can become more invasive and sometimes violent.

As one of the most overlooked zones of protection for your child, aggression at school deserves your close examination and thoughtful, strategic parenting. No one should be permitted to intimidate your child in any fashion. And because you cannot be everywhere at once, your role is not only to defend his boundaries, but to enable him to know and defend them on his own.

HOW TO PROTECT FROM AGGRESSION AT SCHOOL

Role-Play. As before, role-play is one of the most effective methods of dealing with and preventing conflict. See the role-play techniques described above under "Self-Worth" for specific uses of this method. Where you feel unable to coach your child, enlist the help and support of others, or search together for guides on this issue. There are dozens of children's storybooks dedicated to the subject of bullies and aggression at school (parent recommendations are included in the Toolbox). Introduce these periodically into your storytime experience to provide an organic context for discussing these challenges with your child.

Above all, teach your child reactions that fit your comfort zone. If physical self-defense is a violation of your principles, communicate that and help your child devise alternative responses.

Physical Training. A child who *feels* capable of defending himself physically emits an air of confidence that others sense. Therefore, providing your child with physical defense training, such as karate, does much more than equip him with tools to protect himself. Knowing how to fight or deflect an attack makes your child less susceptible to attack, so it is a measure of prevention.

Even if you are uncomfortable with training your child in the art of self-defense, you might consider enlisting him in a physical strengthening activity, such as athletics, yoga or Pilates, as these will define his body in ways that discourage others from aggressing him, with the added benefit of building habits of wellness.

ZONE #3: SIBLING RELATIONSHIPS

Sibling rivalry is a source of great debate. A surprising number of parents believe that it is not only natural for siblings to fight, but healthy. "They need to learn how to work out their differences on their own," I am often told.

However, children are not born with negotiation skills, and few possess the savvy, maturity or life experience to successfully and constructively barter power with their siblings. As a result, in nearly every sibling transaction, there are winners and losers; and the winner generally wins while the loser always loses.

WHY SIBLINGS FIGHT

The results of sibling struggles are not determined so much by the child's age or physical strength as by unconscious acts of bias and attention in parents' reactions to those struggles. In fact, most sibling rivalries center on determining who owns the reliable attention (a.k.a. protection) of one or more of the parents.

Parents often do not realize that they have triggered sibling conflict with subtle displays of preference and favoritism. If the sister aggresses her brother and goes unpunished by the parent, then the sister gains power, both by dominating her brother and by achieving the passive sanction of the parent. If the sister *is* punished, she gains the parent's angry attention (which she was probably seeking), while the brother receives sympathetic coddling (which he was probably seeking). One child learns to gain attention as a dominator; the other as a victim.

When parents take a "hands off" approach to sibling rivalry, they are providing unspoken support to whomever prevails. The victim then grows resentful of the parent's failure to protect, and the victor becomes emboldened by what appears to be the parent's solid endorsement. In their ensuing struggles, the victim must resort to his primal instincts—fight or flight. There is no opportunity for discussion and concession because consensus-building requires a neutral and safe territory.

HOW SIBLINGS LEVERAGE POWER

Without a system of protection and a plan for fairness, each sibling will instinctively draw from his power source (the parent with whom he is most aligned) to assert some level of control over the other siblings. He may also use physical attacks, sabotage or passive aggressive behaviors to gain the upper hand.

If you are a sibling, chances are that you were either the "winner" (conqueror, intimidator, surrogate mom, brown-noser) or the "loser" (victim, baby, tattle-tale) in your sibling struggles, and that you have carried that role with you into adulthood and into your interactions with others. Is it possible that much of the dysfunction in relationships today stems from the patterns formed on the sibling battleground?

Sibling relationships play a key role in the life choices children make and the types of relationships they shape for themselves. Victimization by one's siblings or the experience of dominating them can lock both winner and loser into constrained identity patterns that affect their relationships with friends, mates, colleagues, and ultimately with their own children.

HOW TO PROTECT SIBLINGS

Fairness Plan. A fairness plan is a set of rules governing behavior among siblings and between parents and siblings. The best way to develop this plan is to talk through several scenarios of conflict that occur frequently among you and between the siblings. Analyze those scenarios together, reflecting on how the conflict arises and alternatives that would foster more harmony and cooperation.

For example, a family I worked with wanted to address the constant battling among their three children, ranging from 4-16 years of age. The parents realized that their biased treatment of the children was contributing to overall family strife, so they decided to create a policy that would make the rules of engagement clear to everyone in the family.

They held three meetings. In the first, everyone in the family (even the four-year-old) generated questions about how the family functions. The children offered questions like "Who gets to choose what we watch on TV?" and "How old do you have to be to have a cell phone?" The parents generated questions like, "How will we react when one of the children tells on the other?" and "What is our policy about age and privilege among the siblings?"

NAMING YOUR GAME

Why not choose a word or coin a phrase that is uniquely fitting to the type of family communication you would like to have? For example, you could call your meeting a rap session, powwow, think tank, huddle, rendezvous or rally. Perhaps even create your own family brand of communication, like the Peterson Powwow or Gonzalez Group-Think. Branding your family practices and traditions enhances your child's sense of identity and belonging.

A week later, they met again to share and discuss the answers that everyone gave to the questions they had generated in the last meeting. To help the four-year-old, the eldest sibling took dictation to record his answers for the meeting. There was debate, but it was focused on giving each family member an opportunity to react to ideas.

They took one week more to reflect and think about their discussion, and then came together one last time to finalize their policy.

As is often the case with families I encounter, the children were completely engaged and supportive, offering thoughtful and insightful answers that generated a policy that the entire family respected.

MEETING ROLES

Here are some suggestions for roles that contribute to a productive, constructive and loving family meeting. Of course, smaller families will need fewer roles, but always have a leader.

Leader – Launches the first meeting; suggests protocol; suggests an agenda and ensures inclusion of others' needs on the agenda; synthesizes the results of consensus-building into a decision; suggests ways to resolve a disagreement.

Love Captain – Attends to the emotional needs of each participant; suggests ways to make the meeting more loving and tender; makes note of behavior that violates the "love code."

Timekeeper – Notes the time; ensures that the meeting starts and ends on time; keeps speakers aware of their time limits.

Peacekeeper – Uses body language (i.e., standing, raised hand, lowered head) to silence the group when discussion goes astray or individuals cannot be heard.

Goalie – Monitors the goals of the meeting and ensures that they are all addressed; keeps the group from going outside the scope of the goals set at the beginning of the meeting.

Children are so exhilarated by meaningful opportunities to participate in our world that when they do, they are usually inclined to bring their best thinking to the table. I am regularly impressed with the brilliance of children who are invited to help solve family problems.

For example, the eldest in one family suggested a rotational "buddy system" he had learned at camp, in which family members would be paired as buddies, with the job of providing proactive support and encouragement to each other, and then switch partners from month to month. They drew names from a hat to decide who would be partnered with whom. The system worked beautifully, because it raised the consciousness level of each family member, clarified roles, and dissolved territorial alliances that had formed over time.

For some, this approach to family may seem foreign or impractical. However, the power of this visionary approach is that it draws from the ingenuity of each stakeholder in the family. Rather than building a solution based solely on traditional practice or on what others around them have done, this family chose to look within itself and devise a solution that is informed by the needs and perspectives of each member of the family. In doing so, this family not only solved their immediate problem, but they built stronger relationships in the process.

WHY FAIRNESS PLANS WORK

Ultimately, creating a fairness plan is as much about the process as it is about the final product. In this process, everyone is heard, even the children contribute, important issues are discussed, and decisions are made through consensus.

Zone #4: Predators

It is undeniable that children today are more vulnerable to threat from strangers through the Internet, as a result of the fragmentation of communities, and due to the increased number of activities children and parents schedule day-to-day. There is less face time between parent and child today, and there are fewer known and trusted faces in a community.

While the reality may be difficult to absorb, you can safely assume that your child has been or will be approached by a predator, either online or in person. Therefore, it is your duty to prepare your child for this experience, even if doing so makes you uncomfortable.

The New Technological Social Order

The presence of computers and the Internet has spurred a monumental transfer of power from adult to child. Prior to the Internet, adults controlled most factors of their children's social interactions: where, when, how and with whom.

The Internet has given children the power to interact with one another and with adults, across all social, cultural, and national boundaries, without the knowledge or permission of their parents. This capability has happened too quickly for society to develop a means for protecting children who use the Internet, and adults have too little time or know-how to keep pace with their children's seemingly effortless proficiency.

The result is a new and rapidly evolving social order in which children have access to a powerful tool for which they have little modeling and supervision. Today, a child can see some of the most violent, sexual and morally repugnant realities of the adult world; but because parents are either ignorant of or uncertain how to manage their children's Internet activity, children are likely to continue its use unseen and unprotected.

Find support for you and your child in safe use of the Internet at *www.netsmartz.org.*

There is more to preparation than simply protecting your child. If your child is approached by a predator, in person or online, and has not had preparation for the experience, he will sense that a threat exists outside of your control. He will doubt your ability to protect him because the predator was able to access him without your knowing. Because you did not prepare him, he assumes that you are unaware of this threat.

Remember that young children internalize blame for harm they suffer, so if your child is preyed upon, he is unlikely to alert you because he feels embarrassed and responsible for the threat. He fears the predator, but he also fears your judgment, and so he may act out to get more of your protective attention, while concealing the true reason for wanting it.

How To Protect From Predators

To protect your child from predators, use one or more of the techniques described below. I recommend using them all in sequence, varying your approach based on your comfort level and the age of your child. If you have a **Lunchbox Age** or **Telephone Age** child, I recommend building a plan and strategy together with him, inviting his ownership of the entire process. Remember to use images (i.e., storybooks and drawings) when communicating with young children (you will find tips and resources listed in the Toolbox).

Presence. Your child is vulnerable to predators when he is alone, unsupervised, or being supervised by someone other than you. Make a list of all of these times.

If at all possible, make random, unannounced visits to locations where your child may be vulnerable during these times. By doing so, you show your child, and those who supervise or spend time with him, that you are ever-present, watchful and actively protecting him.

If your child is of **Telephone Age**, he may complain or criticize your tactic. Ignore him. He has to complain to save face with his friends. But as long as you discuss your approach with him in advance so that he can anticipate your actions, he will secretly welcome this protection.

YOU HAVE THE RIGHT TO INQUIRE

Before you visit your child during a supervised time, make a list of questions you would like to ask those who supervise him. The purpose of asking questions is primarily to establish that you are watching and thinking consciously about the care of your child. You are discreetly putting his caregivers on notice.

Some suggestions for questions include: "What were you doing before this job?" "How long have you worked here?" "Do you have children of your own?" "What made you choose this line of work?"

If you are worried about offending someone, don't be. While it is important that your child's caregivers like you and your child, it is more important that they have respect for and adhere to your expectations for his care. It is your right and your duty to protect him at all cost.

Adults who have access to your child, and who might otherwise be inclined to neglect, abuse or prey on your child, are less inclined to do so if they feel you are aggressively involved in his life. If you are seldom seen, your child is more vulnerable. Predators often observe their prey before making an attack; so if you are present unpredictably and with some frequency, you provide a strong disincentive for them to target your child.

Research. Know your enemy. Alone, or together with your child, research the dangers of predators and their behaviors. Your goal is to better understand what your child may encounter and to prepare him as best you can. Use books, news accounts, the Internet, and organizations whose mission is to prevent children from falling victim to predators, such as the National Center for Missing and Exploited Children (www.missingkids. com).

PREDATOR-PROOFING A WOBBLY AGE CHILD

You may find it uncomfortable to role-play predator scenarios with your **Wobbly Age** child. Perhaps you believe that he will be traumatized by the experience or that you will cause him unnecessary anxiety. Not so.

Your wobbly one is attuned to danger on a subconscious level. He simply cannot articulate his awareness to you because he does not yet have the emotional or linguistic sophistication. However, you need look no further than popular children's books to discover that children are drawn to themes associated with danger. One simple approach to predator-proofing a **Wobbly Age** child is to use the storybooks you already read together (i.e., Little Red Riding Hood) to discuss reactions to predators and ways to avoid danger.

Rest assured, your child will feel nothing but comfort and relief at the opportunity to discuss and act out potentially dangerous situations in the safety of your guidance and support.

Role-Play. By now you have read several suggestions for role-play and are familiar with its purpose, design and benefits. Apply those reenactment methods here to prepare your child for potential encounters with predators.

Online Role-Play. Because much of modern predator behavior occurs online, it is important that you take your role-play to that domain, so that your child is prepared for the types of approaches and invitations he will receive from strangers through sites he is likely to use, such as www.myspace.com. To provide your child with coaching in handling online predators, consult organizations like The NetSmartz Workshop (www. netsmartz.org).

If you have a **Lunchbox Age** or **Telephone Age** child and do not believe that he is spending time on sites like www.myspace.com, or if you are resistant to voluntarily showing such sites to him, think again. It is inevitable that your child will learn about those sites; and if you are not the person that introduces them to him, he will feel less confident about your guidance. He is likely to infer from your naïveté (feigned or genuine) that you do not know the information that he finds valuable and that others who do know it are in a better position to provide leadership. He may, therefore, steer away from your guidance and seek it from those who initially drew him to those sites.

Commit emergency information to memory. Does your child know to call 911 in an emergency, and does he know the phone numbers of family members and neighbors? Does he know his address? Your work address? Does he know where to find public phones or help along the routes he uses? Children as young as age three are capable of memorizing substantial amounts of data. If you incorporate data into songs or rhymes, it will be easier to remember in a crisis moment. Imagine him running from a predator and needing to tell someone your phone number. Incorporate this memorized data into your role-play. For more guidance on preparing your child for emergencies, see the resources listed in the Toolbox.

Establish physical boundaries. Your child should have a clear sense of boundaries in relation to his body so that he can recognize when someone is invading his space, attempting to touch him inappropriately or abduct him.

Find a class, book or video that provides instruction for children in how to physically respond to a predator (I have listed books and videos in the Toolbox). Then practice scenarios with those physical defense techniques as part of your role-play.

ZONE #5: IMAGINARY THREATS

When your child fears ghosts or monsters, or suspects that dark forces are lurking in his closet or under the bed, he is likely communicating a need for protection. He may truly believe that ghosts and monsters lurk just beyond the bed skirt, but what he is feeling is a lack of protection. However, without the ability to articulate this feeling, he projects fear and vulnerability and invents threats.

The important aspect of the ghost or monster is that it is an invisible force; therefore, you cannot protect him from it unless you stay extremely close and vigilant. The ghost/monster can also represent a force that the child feels is out of your reach. Often, when a child is being emotionally or physically threatened outside of the home, such as by a bully or a predator, a ghost or monster will appear in the home.

HOW TO PROTECT FROM IMAGINARY THREATS

Role-Play + Presence. Because your child's fear of ghosts or monsters probably indicates fear of a threat outside your reach, you can employ some of the same techniques described earlier regarding discouraging predators, such as establishing a presence in locations and during times when your child may feel vulnerable.

To target the potential threat more strategically, visit the library or bookstore and bring home age-appropriate books that address typical childhood threats, such as bullies and predators, and introduce these into your storytime. Children do not typically respond to direct questioning about a threat they are experiencing, but they are highly responsive when asked questions in the context of a story, drawing, or theatrical reenactment.

For this reason, books, drawing and role-play are commonly used by police, medical professionals and psychologists who want to communicate with children about troubling issues. By using the same tools, you may be able to identify the threat and know where to target your presence. The Toolbox provides detailed guidance on effectively communicating with your child through role-play.

Reliable Attention. Your child may not be under threat, but may be seeking predictable attention (protection) from you, using ghosts and monsters to draw you near. If you believe that attention is your child's motivation, apply the techniques outlined earlier in this chapter, such as committing small, reliable amounts of time to your child. His behavior should subside after the third or fourth fulfilled commitment.

In these last two chapters, we focused on your child's need for attention and for protection from outside forces. We looked at how you can respond to his behavioral cues when he needs protection and how you can proactively enhance his safety without waiting for those cues.

Before we leave the issue of protection, however, there is one last important element in a parent's protective role that is often misinterpreted and misdirected. In the next chapter, we will explore how the need to protect a child can be confused with the need to control and limit a child's experience. We will also look at methods parents can use to evaluate and redirect controlling tendencies.

Chapter Six
Control and Criticism

Parental instinct can be controlling and fearful. Worried about your child's safety and the consequences of her decisions, you may find yourself holding her back, sheltering her from potential danger, limiting her social experiences, or screening her information. Are these natural reactions? Yes. Are they healthy? No.

The type of protection that will yield a closer parent-child bond and a lifetime of mutual respect is that which does not shield the child from danger, but coaches her for it. Preparing her by proactively educating her about potential challenge, conflict, or danger positions you as her ally, her confidante, and her source of information and power. In taking this approach, you also preempt the influence of those who could otherwise lead her astray.

Protection Versus Control

Control is when you consistently restrain your toddler's movement. *Protection* is when you provide ample environments and opportunities for your toddler to move freely and teach her to recognize voice and hand signals for when she needs to come closer.

Control is when you take rights away from your child as a form of punishment. *Protection* is when you implement a system of increasingly challenging responsibilities through which she can prove herself capable and reliable.

Control is when you forbid your child from seeing her friend, because you fear her friend's values (or lack of values). *Protection* is when you meet with her friend's family, with your child present, share your concerns openly and communicate your expectations and boundaries for their interactions.

Control is when you forbid your child to date. *Protection* is when you introduce dating as a topic before your child is compelled to want it, and then discuss and role-play dating scenarios and even establish a dating timeline based on mutual agreement.

> Control is a cave. Protection is *armor.*

Notes from the Animal Kingdom

If you have observed the behavior of animals in the wild, you may share my view that some animals are considerably less obsessive about the behavior of their children than we humans. Does the lioness prevent her cubs from trying (and sometimes failing) to execute the skills that she performs each day? Does she keep them secluded from the world of "eat or be eaten?"

No, she and a host of other mammals expose their young to real opportunities to practice life skills as early as possible, merging them into the patterns of adult living as they show competency. The parents are ever watchful, guarding their children from danger, but they never let protection interfere with the goal of independence. In fact, they protect *solely for the purpose of promoting risk-taking* behaviors in their children.

What can we learn from our mammalian friends? It is that good parenting—that which ensures the successful growth and maturation of a child—is achieved through a balance of empowerment and protection.

In essence, control is a reactive mechanism that restricts, suppresses and limits your child. Protection is a proactive mechanism that embraces the inevitable challenges your child will face in life and defines the rules of engagement she will use to navigate unfamiliar terrain.

Protective parenting grounds your child in the values and belief systems of the family, making it more likely that she will be guided by those values in her interactions. Conversely, parenting driven by control will turn your child away from your values, because she will associate those values with limitations rather than power.

THE CRITICAL PARENT AND CONTROL

Parents have a natural inclination to criticize their children. After all, you send your child out into the world to represent you—your belief systems, moral standards, biases and personal views. Your parenting is exposed through your child on a daily basis, so it is only natural that you would feel a compulsion to monitor her behavior carefully and let her know when you disapprove.

We must address criticism, though, because it does affect your relationship with your child and her sense of the emotional safety your care provides. Left unchecked, critical parenting can spur some of a child's most destructive behaviors. So, in this section, we will take a close look at criticism, recognizing that it is something with which nearly all parents struggle.

Criticism is a close relative of control. Often without realizing it, a critical parent will undermine a child's self-confidence with the subconscious intent of preventing her from venturing too far from the fold. While this is not a healthy approach, it is an effective one. A child riddled with self-doubt is not likely to take many risks or feel bold enough to challenge a parent's authority.

If, for example, you have a **Lunchbox Age** or **Telephone Age** child, and you feel that she does not make a positive impression on others when being introduced—that her posture is poor, her verbal skills weak, her eye contact evasive, or her appearance sloppy—you may be inclined to point these flaws out to her as she prepares for a social encounter. Noting her inadequacies makes her self-conscious and averse to any opportunities that could end in failure.

A parent who criticizes in this way is probably fearful about the child's growing independence, and insecure about her ability to take care of herself or defend herself. Because of this critical-protective approach, the child will potentially grow to believe that she is inadequate and will become increasingly reliant on the parent's judgment. She will become frozen by the criticism, hesitant to act without approval or signs of confidence from her parent.

Most parents who take this judgmental approach to

raising their children do so as a learned behavior that has been passed from one generation to another. To make matters worse, many of those who had critical parents not only continue to live under their censure, but watch as their own children are subjected to the same judgmental approaches by their grandparents. The cycle of criticism is given new life.

For example, one of the families I worked with was a married couple with two children, one of **Wobbly Age** and one of **Lunchbox Age**. The mother's parents were highly critical when it came to the children's eating habits, and often made an issue of this in front of the entire family at dinner, insisting that the children eat what they resisted eating, and pressuring the mother to do something about the children's resistance. In dinner table scenarios like these, not only is the self-esteem of the children under attack, but that of their parents— the child's source of power and protection—as well. Grandparents who openly criticize their grandchildren or, worse, their children's parenting methods, are doing double the damage by making the children feel insecure and the parents appear powerless.

We are not here to analyze family history, but it is important for parents with critical tendencies to recognize that those tendencies are probably part of a generational cycle that can and should be broken.

Are You Critical or Correcting?

Criticism is often confused with correction, but there is a distinction. When a parent shows a child how to write the letter "e" correctly, that is not criticism. When a parent whispers "remember to say 'thank you'" in the child's ear, that is not criticism. When a parent tells a child that a "C" grade is unacceptable, that is not criticism.

Criticism is a personal judgment that has a hurtful effect, attacking a child's self-esteem, such as when a parent says:

> "You are too skinny."
> "Your handwriting is sloppy."
> "Your friends are delinquents."
> "You are lazy."
> "Your grammar is poor."

You can determine if your behavior is critical by checking your motivation. If you address your child's actions or skills out of embarrassment, anger or worry, you are probably being critical. If, instead, your intent is to prepare your child for a challenge, mentor her in a new skill, or help her adapt to your family's creed and practices, you are probably providing correction.

How To Address Critical Parenting

If you think you might be practicing critical parenting and would like to break the cycle, here are a few techniques that have worked for other parents (and grandparents!):

Journal. Being critical of your children can be such an integral part of your relationship with them that you may have difficulty isolating the moments when criticism begins and ends. Journaling can help with this. If you are not one for writing things down, consider using an audio recorder for a week or two, making a concerted effort to record voice notes to yourself after an incident in which you felt you were being critical. Invite your spouse or partner to make journal entries as well. If your child is of **Lunchbox Age** or **Telephone Age**, invite her to do the same.

Identify your hot spots and target them. Recruit your spouse or partner, a close friend or relative, or even your child (if she is of **Lunchbox Age** or **Telephone Age**). With their help, identify one or two scenarios in which you have been guilty of critical behavior. Do you have a tendency to criticize your child when you are under pressure yourself? When your parents are near? When your child displays a certain habit? Most parents have "hot spots" like these that trigger critical attitudes.

Once you know your hot spots, identify the force that is compelling you to be critical. For example, if you tend to criticize your child's writing skills, what you want is for her writing to improve. Criticism will not yield those results, but equipping her for improvement will.

Now take yourself through some tough self-analysis. Examine how you currently support your child's growth in this area. If you are relying on her teacher to fill the gap in her ability, then direct your criticism there. If you have hired a tutor to help her, but you are unhappy with your child's progress, direct your attention to the tutor or find a replacement.

Have you modeled technique for your child? Shopped for guides with her? Encouraged and facilitated her increased exposure to reading, writing and language use in general? If writing is important to you, then build opportunities for the two of you to do it together, in work and in play.

Your child, no matter her age, cares just as much about her writing as you do. However, if you have had judgmental reactions to her attempts at writing, then she has likely begun to internalize the belief that she cannot succeed in that area.

TUTORS AND DEPENDENCY

Parents with concerns about a child's academic performance will often seek a tutor. Perhaps the parent does not know the subject well enough or have the time to help, or perhaps the child is significantly behind in a skill. In some cases, a tutor is provided to prepare a child for a challenge to come.

However, the decision to hire a tutor is one that can have deleterious effects on the child if not handled properly. In many instances, tutoring can be perceived by the child as the parent's "quiet criticism" or way of saying "You can't succeed without help."

Certain approaches to tutoring can promote the child's dependence and reinforce the child's belief that she cannot learn a certain subject on her own. A child who has struggled with an academic challenge, only to then be enlightened by a tutor, feels an intense relief that can become addictive. She may be less inclined to build skill in that area if she knows that she can rely on a tutor to relieve her if she falters again.

How can you avoid this problem? First, by being actively involved in the selection and monitoring of the tutor. Insist that the tutor provide general coaching in broad skill sets coupled with infrequent (weekly or monthly) check-ins that allow your child to demonstrate proficiency without relying on day-to-day help. Choose a tutor that teaches independent learning, and sit in on one or two sessions so that you become a more powerful (and less critical) source of support.

Establish a signal system. Signal systems are predetermined signals that carry meaning for those using and observing them. In this case, the signal is devised to provide family members with a way to communicate quickly and comfortably when they feel subjected to criticism.

Signals are incredibly effective with children, and in relationships in general, because they do not require sophisticated communication skills, they provide immediate relief for the "target," and they give the offender an instant, but civil, prompting that usually quells the behavior peacefully.

Some examples of simple physical signals that anyone in the family can use include: a raised hand, a lowered head, or palms together (a universal symbol of pacification). Consider establishing different symbols for distinct behaviors or emotions. See more on signals and signs in the Toolbox.

Therapy. If you do not see results from any of the above techniques, I strongly recommend that you consider family therapy. This should be a family decision, as it will take everyone's cooperation and investment in the solutions recommended by the therapist. For deep-seated issues that are layered or distorted, family therapy can provide mechanisms for healing, growth and life enhancement. Therapy usually requires a significant investment of time on everyone's part, but the benefits endure throughout your lifetime and are carried forward in all of your child's future relationships and her parenting.

If you are considering therapy but not yet prepared to invest the time or expense, I recommend reading *Getting the Love You Want: A Guide for Couples* by Dr. Harville Hendrix. Despite the implications of the title, this is an invaluable resource for anyone who wishes to better understand how childhood shapes adult behaviors and relationships. This book has been transformative for me and for many of the parents and child professionals I have known.

We now leave our discussion of your child's need for protection to explore the third and last P, prediction. As we move ahead, you will begin to see more clearly the relationship among the three P's. You will notice that both power and protection play a role in the next section. In fact, you will see that prediction is a fusion of the first two P's. When your child feels that she can rely on you, anticipate and prepare for challenges, and become a stakeholder in decisions made about her own future, she is both powerful and protected.

Part Three

Prediction

Chapter Seven
Power of Predictability

It is a simple oversight in parenting that we do not keep our children in the loop on the direction of their lives. It starts at birth. Because our infant cannot communicate intelligibly, we develop the notion that children are not sophisticated enough to receive information about their destinies.

We decide what they will eat, what they will wear, when they will get up and go to bed, when they will watch television, what activities and hobbies they will pursue, when they will be allowed to date and drive, and so many facets of their lives...largely without ever consulting them.

We plan their lives and ours, but seldom do we involve them in those plans. We go on vacation, move to a new city or home, have more children, and separate or divorce, but seldom are children made aware of the impending circumstances of those decisions in advance. They usually get last-minute notification and have little to say about the situation. And we think this is the way it is supposed to be.

Yet, as a child approaches adolescence, we expect him to start exercising sound judgment and decision-making skills as he acquires the privileges and responsibilities of driving, dating, working, choosing a field of study and then a career.

But after having been kept out of decision-making processes for most of his life, how will he then suddenly know how a decision is made? He has had so few opportunities to make decisions for himself and to be part of those made in the family. His primary responsibility has been to obey orders; now he will need to navigate life-altering decisions on his own. It does not have to be this way. You can change that today with some of the simple measures outlined below.

BUILDING A PREDICTABLE LIFE

Your child has healthy predictability when he can reliably anticipate how you and other family members will react to him and to one another, what opportunities he will have, and what challenges he will face. Therefore, in considering methods for offering your child more predictability, let us look at three areas of his life where it matters most: your family's behavior; your schedules and routines; and preparing for what's to come.

FAMILY BEHAVIOR

Some families have relatively predictable patterns, and others have haphazard and ever-changing systems for functioning. If you feel that your family consists more of individuals acting of their own accord with little agreement about the rules of behavior and day-to-day functions, then consider giving your family's behavior more structure by defining the rules of your interactions more clearly. Your child will be comforted by clarity about expectations and protocol.

A family policy includes statements about what your family values most, how you interact with each other and with those outside your fold, and the family's vision and goals for the future. Of course, your family policy can contain anything you choose to put in it, and the more participation you have from your children, the more authenticity your policy will have. On the next page, I have provided some questions to help you start.

Consider having a family meeting to develop your policy and ensure that all members of the family have a chance to offer input. If you would like support for holding an effective family meeting, see the workbook companion to this book, *The Three P's of Parenting: Family Workbook*.

SCHEDULING AND ROUTINES

Families today find it more challenging to function predictably because life and family structure are more complex. A modern family is likely to include parents with demanding career paths, children from more than one marriage, shared custody agreements, and participation in an assortment of extracurricular activities.

QUESTIONS TO HELP YOU CREATE A FAMILY POLICY

TIME

- How do we start, spend and end our workdays?
- How do we start, spend and end our days off?
- What are our life priorities? (work, family, self, etc.)

TRADITIONS

- What traditions do we value most? Why?
- How do we observe holidays and special days?
- What traditions would we like to have?

PUBLIC BEHAVIOR

- How do we behave with friends?
- How do we behave with polite strangers?
- How do we dress for casual experiences, for professional occasions, for formal occasions?

PRIVATE BEHAVIOR

- How are children expected to behave toward their parents?
- How are parents expected to behave toward their children?
- How do we respect each other's need for privacy?
- How do we help and take care of each other?
- How do we deal with anger, resentment, fear, and worry?

HOUSEHOLD

- What are the roles in the household, who has them, and why?
- How do we maintain the look and feel of the home?

However, there are ways that even the most complex family can build routines that allow a child to move smoothly through each day, knowing what to do and when, feeling prepared for the experiences he will have and the challenges he will face. Having a level of certainty about his day, week or month soothes a child, who often feels a sense of helplessness because of his dependence on others.

I recommend a quick assessment of the existing routines in your child's life to identify where there is certainty and predictability and where those may be lacking. Start small and build, looking at his days, then weeks and months.

Use the "everyday task" list that I introduced in Chapter One as a starting point, and ask yourself "How predictable is the timing of each of these tasks? Is it always clear how and when they should be done?" Think about the anchoring routines in your child's life, like waking up and going to bed, eating, and togetherness with you. What about your weekend routines? Does your child know what to expect from day to day? Week to week? Month to month?

As you think through your child's routines, give consideration to the timing of activities, how you expect those activities to be done, and who is responsible for doing them. Here is some guidance in thinking through these factors:

Timing. Your child's routines do not have to be identical from day to day; they only need to be predictable. For instance, your child may have a routine for doing homework on Tuesday and Thursday, but a different routine for homework on Monday and Wednesday. A pattern is a pattern, no matter how complex it is, and complexity is better than unpredictability.

Families with complicated work and play schedules can use timing patterns to build routines that work for everyone and provide children with the level of predictability they need to be functioning, contributing members of the family.

Methods. Children want to know *exactly* how tasks should be done, and they want nothing more than to do those tasks to your satisfaction. Therefore, when introducing routines into your child's life, a key factor in your success is in the extent to which you model how things are done.

Roles. The bigger your family and the more complex your needs, the more critical it is that everyone, your child included, has responsibilities for making the routine work. Roles matter, and the clearer they are, the happier everyone is.

PREDICTION STARTS EARLY

If you have a **Wobbly Age** or **Lunchbox Age** child, consider including him in conversations and planning sessions where decisions about rules and schedules are discussed. Invite his suggestions and allow him to witness how consensus is built and decisions are made.

As he grows in his ability to contribute to discussions like these and demonstrates responsibility, expand his powers and opportunities for leadership.

Family meetings are perfect opportunities for exposing your young child to planning and prediction. You can never start too early, and you will be surprised at the level of maturity he can exhibit. Use the communication tips provided in the Toolbox to engage him and build his participation.

I worked with a couple that wanted to solve the problem of their three children fighting over use of a shared bathroom every morning and evening. This problem was destructive to the whole family, disrupting peace at the start and end of each day.

The problem? There was no routine. None of the children knew who would use the bathroom, nor when or how. They would fight to be first, hurry one another, and, in their haste, create a mess and start the day with ill will. The youngest, least able to defend his rights, typically went last, finding the space in total disarray and understocked, requiring him to seek help from his parents in order to finish his routine. To make matters worse, the delay in getting to the bathroom was causing the youngest to go to bed too late, making him tired and prone to outbursts in the morning.

The parents spent two nights watching the spectacle and taking notes. Then, they compared notes and designed a system that accounted for timing, sequence, needs, supplies, and procedures. They walked their children through their individual routines, and then they brought the siblings together for dress rehearsal.

After a week and some tweaking here and there by the parents, the system for bathroom use worked flawlessly, and the children enjoyed the challenge of keeping it that way. Ultimately, something as simple as using a shared space resulted in better familial relationships and modeling of successful life habits for the children.

ATTENTION ROUTINES

Routines also apply to your together time. In Chapter Four, I encouraged you to make feasible, reliable commitments of attention to your child. If he can predict when, where and how he will see you, his mind is eased, and he is less likely to use behavior to get your attention. It is not necessary for you to alter your life drastically in order to offer your child this level of predictability. Your child is not as concerned with the amount of your attention as with its dependability.

CALENDARS

With **Wobbly**, **Lunchbox**, and **Telephone Age** children, I recommend that you use a calendar to plan and communicate family events. A calendar is particularly powerful for a child because it offers a concrete visual reference of time, a concept that younger children often struggle to understand.

A calendar not only offers your child a visual prediction tool; it offers him a model of planning and organization that can be applied to many aspects of his life. In larger families, a calendar can improve communication and prevent conflict. Consider having more than one calendar, dedicating one to daily routines (blocks of time for togetherness, "me" time, meals, TV, storytime, etc.) and one for events.

Remember to use imagery with young children to clarify the meaning of words you say and write. Today, there are dozens of visually-based calendars, from preprinted varieties, to dry-erase and Internet calendars.

For **Wobbly Age** children, I recommend starting with the *My First Daily Planner* by Leaps and Bounds® (www.leapsandbounds.com). As your child moves into **Lunchbox Age**, consider making your own calendars with chart paper or large dry-erase boards. Making a calendar (drawing lines, counting spaces, numbering and naming days) helps a child learn the meaning of each component of a calendar and how to use it. After several opportunities to help you create a monthly calendar, your **Lunchbox Age** child will be able to do this task independently.

For a child in late **Lunchbox Age** or any part of **Telephone Age**, online calendars are ideal because they permit your child to create multiple calendars, one for each key segment of his life, and then share and coordinate single events or entire calendars with you, other family members, friends and even teachers and coaches.

COMMUNICATION ABOUT THE FUTURE

DISCLOSING BAD NEWS

A parent who hides bad news from a child does so to protect the child from anxiety, fear, or grief, but may also want to deny or postpone his own discomfort in confronting the issue with the child. However, it is virtually impossible to hide bad news from your child, because he is so highly skilled in reading your body language.

Children *know* when things are not as they should be. Your child has been watching you carefully since birth. He knows your body language down to the way you blink your eyes, tap your finger, and shift your weight. By the time you are thinking about whether or not to divulge unpleasant news, he already senses that something is wrong.

Withholding information from your child erodes his trust in you and establishes a dynamic in which he not only expects you to conceal or misrepresent the truth, but learns to behave that way himself. By withholding bad news, you are modeling a behavior that he will carry forward, learning to "protect" you by withholding information rather than bonding and confiding in you with trust.

The hardest part of sharing bad news with your child is initiating the conversation. Give yourself a deadline for breaking the news, and ask your spouse or partner, close friend or relative to help you meet that deadline with loving nudges, if necessary. Use one of the resources found in the Toolbox for discussing crisis issues such as divorce or death.

PLANNING FOR THE INEVITABLE

You can predict nearly all of the key experiences your child will have in his youth, the challenges he will face, and the desires he will have. Why? Because you were young once, too.

You know, for example, that at some point your **Lunchbox Age** child will likely want a pet, be rejected by a friend, encounter a bully, struggle in school, ask to attend a sleepover, beg for a Gameboy, lose a competition, and whine "Are we there yet?" from the backseat of the car.

You know that your **Telephone Age** child will be influenced by peer pressure, and all too soon will be coming to you begging for the latest trendy item or special privilege that his peers have been flaunting. He will test his boundaries and challenge your rules when it comes to his school work, phone, curfew, driving, dating, and use of alcohol and drugs.

These issues come as no surprise, so use this to your parenting advantage. Think through what is to come, how you would like to prepare your child for it and how you would like to manage the situation when it occurs.

Chances are that you gave considerable time and energy to planning for the birth or adoption of your child. You probably read books, took classes and even restructured your career and personal life to accommodate the new arrival. Planning and setting the stage for your child's transition to adulthood is just as important. The more prepared you are for what is to come, the better positioned you will be to nurture and prepare him.

Preemptive Dialogue

The key to preventing some of the most common challenges of parenting Telephone Age children is in preempting the conflict caused by peer pressure by initiating dialogue about key issues in advance.

What typically happens to a Telephone Age child is that he hears his peers bragging about or longing for a privilege—such as getting a cell phone, going on dates, or driving—and runs home to demand it. And because the parent has made no preparations for this demand, has not built consensus with the spouse or partner, and has not already broached the issue with the child, the parent will be easily positioned as the evil dictator who is denying the child's rights.

The stage is then set for the child to challenge, and perhaps overthrow, the parent's decision by aligning with his peers. A cycle is set in motion in which the parent must prove who is boss, and the child must prove the parent wrong.

On average, you should be discussing future decisions with your child one to two years before the *desire* will manifest, not one to two years before the privilege is expected. For instance, you will find it easier to engage your child at age 8 to 10 on the topic of one day having a cell phone, than to wait for him to begin demanding it at age 13 when his peers instigate a confrontation. If a child can legally drive at age 15, then his peer group will be talking and plotting by age 14, which means that you should be discussing the issue with him by age 12 or 13. You do not have to make a decision at that age. It just means that you are talking actively and with mutual respect about the pros and cons and responsibilities of that privilege.

When you discuss future privileges before your child has a desire for them, you dilute the power of his peer group. If you are the first to bring it up, and you and your child have discussed the matter in an open and consensus-building process, his peer group will have less power to convince the child that you are unfair or not on his side.

Now, let us take the idea of prediction in parenting to a higher level. In the next chapter, I will show you not only how to build predictability into your child's life, but how to do so while helping him find purpose, direction and avenues for expressing his unique gifts and talents.

Chapter Eight
A Child's Life, By Design

Prediction-based parenting can do much more than eliminate a child's behavior problems. By engaging your child in a process of envisioning the future, preparing for new experiences and embracing maturity, you imbue her with confidence, purpose, and direction, and equip her for the challenges of peer pressure and critical life decisions.

One of the most effective ways to prepare your child for the future is through life planning. In this process, you help your child begin to identify and explore her interests, passions, and special gifts. Then, you guide her in shaping a vision based on the patterns she discovers in herself. Every child benefits from having a mission and a life plan, starting as early as age 8.

A life plan and sense of purpose are especially critical for children of highly successful parents. Children living in the shadow of parents who are revered by society struggle throughout their lives to shape identities that are distinctly their own. A life plan addresses that problem while building a lasting bond between parent and child.

RAISING A CHILD WITH PURPOSE

We each need to feel that we matter in the lives of others, and even very young children can develop a sense of mission and purpose. Young children understand purpose best when it is deeply personal, such as in the care of a pet. Those in the elementary years will identify with causes that the parent cares about most. And children approaching their tweens and teens will have zest for involvement in larger social movements. In each of these phases, you can help your child explore and define her sense of self and her role in society.

Here are some suggestions for activities that may inspire a sense of purpose and mission in your child.

Wobbly Age. Young children connect most with "purpose" when they are able to visually register its impact on others. For that reason, young children are most likely to respond to activities such as:

- Caring for a pet
- Tending a garden
- Visiting the elderly

Lunchbox Age. Children in elementary school are intensely focused on development of intellectual and physical skills and on becoming as much like you as possible. Hence, these children will be most responsive to activities such as:

- Assuming important household responsibilities
- Accompanying you to social or community functions
- Using intellectual skills (i.e., reading, writing, public speaking, scientific knowledge, leadership) for a cause or family business

Telephone Age. Children age 10 and older are primarily focused on determining where they fit in the social order. They want to do anything that involves alliance with a group, and they identify strongly with causes that fight injustice, such as human and civil rights. Most children this age enjoy having authority.

By the time she enters her tweens, your child will likely have a pattern of interest in certain skill sets, such as writing, performance, building, design, etc. I recommend that you encourage her to develop those skills for real-world purposes that fit the motivations of a child in this age group. Activities that a child in the tweens or teens would respond to include:

- Becoming involved in politics or social activism (i.e., working on a campaign or serving as a legislative intern)
- Advocating on behalf of abused children, abused women, or stray animals
- Taking on an apprenticeship or starting a small business
- Volunteering for (or even founding) a non-profit organization
- Teaching a class on a favorite subject or skill
- Becoming a camp counselor

With a tool like the Internet, and proper guidance in how to use it safely and effectively, your child can extend her transformative reach globally. Encourage her to use this tool as a way to become more involved in the adult dialogue around the cause of her choice.

Family. One of the most bonding experiences you can have as a family is in your activism. Hold a family meeting to choose a common cause or to share experiences from your individual missions. The entire family can volunteer at events like clothing donation drives, community beautification campaigns, and Special Olympics competitions. Consider incorporating a family cause into your travel and vacation plans by visiting a site relevant to your concerns (i.e., rain forest, historic preservation site, adoption agency).

YOUR CHILD'S LIFE PLAN

A life plan is a guide, not a script. No one can expect each of his hopes, dreams and ambitions to unfold as envisioned. The richness of life is that it materializes in unexpectedly circuitous ways.

A life plan is a direction and a set of criteria that your child can use to determine which choices are right for her. So often in life, we confront opportunities and choices feeling doubtful about our decisions. Each road we take makes us wonder what we might have found in those we did not.

In this way, the average college student spins her wheels, vacillating about which major to declare, which course to take, which internship to accept, whether an advanced degree is necessary, what job to pursue, where to live and whether her serious relationship fits into her plans. She is afraid to commit to one interest or another because she is unsure about how the tradeoffs will play out over time.

Indecision at that stage of life is thought to be natural, but is not; it is a byproduct of living an unexamined life. Your child *can* develop a vision for her future that prevents indecision at critical life junctures and improves her chances of being poised and ready for the right opportunity when it knocks.

How To Life Plan With Your Child

A life plan starts with identifying a child's strengths and areas of comfort and confidence. The process works because it is highly personalized, and because in developing it, the child feels special, recognized, and keenly aware of her unique talents and potential.

The process of developing a life plan is as important as the plan itself, so you should not fret about the final product or rush to complete it. Your goal is that throughout the experience, your child feels admired and appreciated for who she is. She must also feel completely free to express desires, dreams, ambitions, and personal visions for herself, no matter how extreme or modest they may seem to you. And your child should have absolute privacy in this process, with no one else present, *especially* siblings.

NOTE: If you do not feel that you have a close relationship with your child, I recommend that you recruit a member of your extended family, a family friend, or an adult your child respects to facilitate the life planning process. The child must trust in the person leading her, and she must not feel judged as she responds honestly to questions.

The steps described below can take less than an hour or many hours. Some children move with speed and certainty, and some are more deliberate. You should expect the process to take time and be prepared to spread it over several days. Life planning is made richer when the child has time to think and reflect.

Step 1: Identify the child's interests. This can seem both obvious and daunting. You know your child's interests, but do you know how to guide her through a reflective process about them?

Make a list together. Prompt your child with questions like "What kind of things do you like to do?" "What are your favorites?" "What would you spend time doing if you could?" "If you had more free time, how would you spend it?" Keep asking open questions.

Be careful to let her responses come naturally and avoid inserting your own observations. Do not suggest specific activities; if necessary, you can facilitate the conversation by mentioning categories, such as sports or art, indoors or outdoors, school, summer, etc.

You might also use open-ended statements, such as: "I am happy when I am (blank)." or "It is fun to (blank)." or "I would enjoy doing (blank) every day." Give her plenty of time to think and respond. And if your child is old enough to write, she should. The less you do, the better.

Nothing is too simple or mundane to put on this list. Add any interest that your child does repeatedly without having to be encouraged. Reading comic books, spending time with grandma, helping clean the house, riding horses, playing certain sports, volunteering. They all count.

At no point in this first step should you or anyone else insert your opinions, preferences or reactions. Life planning is a process in which your child becomes the owner of her fate. All children are susceptible to the opinions of adults, and so any negative or critical reaction from the adult in this process will dilute the power of this exercise significantly.

Step 2: Identify motivations. The next step is to discover the motivations for your child's interests. This is the most fascinating step for parents, because something new is always revealed about the child.

First ask the child to talk about why she likes each activity listed in Step 1. When you ask, she may respond very simply with "because it is fun." For children, *fun* can mean engaging, stimulating, inspirational, or self-affirming. So dig deeper. Press on with more questions, such as: "What makes it fun?" "What makes you want to do it?" "What do you feel when you are doing it?" "What would make it not fun?"

Of course, this kind of discussion is not meant to be an interrogation, but it should involve the two of you documenting what she says, right in front of her eyes. (Remember to use imagery to support understanding for younger children.) Be patient, and be willing to wait a day or two if she loses interest or seems unsure.

After discussing a few activities, you should start to hear her say some things twice. Write those comments down, even if they are repeats of something she has already said. Those repeats will be key to Step 3, and it is important that she be able to see those repeats on paper.

Step 3: Identify patterns in her motivation. Once you feel that you have exhausted Step 2, it is time to analyze the results with your child. Your goal here is to find the patterns in her reasons for liking certain activities. The repeat answers that surfaced in Step 2 should give you strong hints.

Do not offer your analysis first. Give her plenty of time to notice the patterns on her own. You may be surprised at the insight she provides into her own thinking. You are not there to tell her what her patterns are; you are there to help her articulate what she sees.

Be her secretary, and jot down keywords that she generates in this step. Once you feel she has done all of the analysis she can or wants to do, encourage her to review her keywords and narrow them to only *four*. These are her patterns of motivation.

To reduce her list to four keywords, she may have to combine like terms or cross out those that are less important. Here is an example of a keyword list that came out of a life planning session I did with a 10-year-old:

> Adventure
> Physical activity
> Social
> Helping others

This short final list contains essential words that define what intrinsically motivates this child. If an opportunity offers her these features, she will be motivated to invest her time and commit to it, without coercion.

There are deeper implications for identifying the patterns in your child's motivations. They serve as criteria when choosing friends and life partners. That does not mean that the girl who generated the keyword example above will only befriend or date people who are adventurous, but it does help her make judgments about relationships and how her priorities mesh with others. This is particularly important in adolescence, when your child needs those in her peer group to support her goals and direction, or when she needs criteria for choosing a peer group whose priorities and interests mesh well with her own.

When you have completed Step 3, you will have identified the essential components of your child's drive and desire. It may not appear to be that revealing; but if you help her use it properly, it will serve her for the rest of her life in ways that may not be fully apparent now.

What is equally important is that your child will have completed a self-inquiry and empowerment process that spurs her to think differently about herself. She will feel respected and loved for the one-of-a-kind, complex being that she is. If you gain nothing more from life planning than this, it will have been worth your time and effort.

Other subtle benefits of life planning are:

- Your child is empowered with self-confidence and personal vision, which fortifies her for dealing with peer pressure.
- You have positioned yourself as a listener and confidante.
- If you complete this process with siblings, each child will have a unique, but constructive, identity and personal vision that negates many of the issues that fuel sibling rivalry.

ADVANCED LIFE PLANNING

There are additional steps to life planning that involve intricate and challenging problem-solving for your child. These steps are most appropriate for children older than 12. For more information about advanced life planning for teens and college-age children, contact us at LearnGarden (www.learngarden.com) or find tips for advanced life planning in *The Three P's of Parenting: Family Workbook.*

How To Use The Keywords

With your child's list of four keywords (patterns of motivation), there are a host of actions you can take to support their use. Here are a few suggestions appropriate for either **Lunchbox Age** or **Telephone Age** children:

Brainstorm careers. Brainstorm with your child careers that are associated with the four patterns she identified. Encourage her to interview friends, family and acquaintances for their opinions on this. Coach your child to approach this process critically, evaluating careers based on how well they meet her criteria for fulfillment.

START YOUNG

If your child is 10 or older, it is time to have the college-career conversation, because your child will, as early as 10, begin to evaluate the career choices of those around her. She will make assumptions about the benefits of being a fashion model over being a physicist, and you want her to make those assumptions as an educated consumer. Being a microbiologist requires a very different path than being an interior designer, and you want her to understand the decisions she will have to make before she has to make them. This is an example of the power of prediction in a child's life.

Someone will influence her career choices, and who is better positioned than you? There is no need to leave this key role to outsiders. You are, and will always be, her best advocate.

Brainstorm college. After the career exploration, discuss college and the training required for her desired careers. Parents too often take for granted the academic path of their children, which can create conflict when it is time to make the decision. Use your child's career preferences and patterns of motivation as a basis for coaching her in postsecondary training options.

Create a coat of arms. Encourage your child to design a coat of arms that incorporates her four keywords into a design or symbol. Whether or not anyone else ever sees this design, it will be registered permanently in her mind, and will imbue her with confidence if and when her personal vision for herself is scrutinized or challenged.

Unite siblings. If you have siblings, encourage them to share the results of their life plans, finding common ground and means for alliance via those keywords. They have each been made to feel special in the life planning process, so now they are confidently positioned to compare notes with their "competition" and find points of overlapping interest. This activity promotes collaboration among your children that will last well into adulthood. If they each know the vision of the other, they are better positioned to provide mutual support.

Establish home learning centers. Once you have helped your child identify her key motivations, you can support her exploration of related interests through home learning centers. A "learning center" is a space in the home (or a portable kit or project that can be pulled out and put away) that the child operates and controls on his own. Typically, the learning center has a theme that is tied to an area that interests the child, such as gardening, space exploration, finance, geography, cooking, fashion design, soccer, and so on.

The learning center empowers your child with the control of space and activity related to something that matters to her. Among the family members, she builds a reputation as a scholar, instilling her with pride and a sense of purpose.

Occasionally, a learning center leads to a child's deeper and broader commitment to a subject, but at times, her interest may fizzle. Do not be discouraged if she loses interest in a subject, and remember that the purpose of the learning center is exploration. Finding that something does not interest her can be a "road sign" for your child on her path toward self-actualization. For your part, all that matters is that she is encouraged to pursue the interests reflected in her life planning process, and that her choices are facilitated, within reason.

A learning center can be quite simple and the benefits immeasurable. A center could be as large as your backyard or as small as your windowsill. After setup and some modeling, the child controls that space, what goes there, and how it is used. A learning center can accommodate any child above the age of 2; all that changes is the basic design and materials provided.

Here are some examples of learning centers:

- Section of the backyard used as a **biosphere** study zone.
- Wall in one of the common areas used to post findings from recent family **energy consumption** study.
- Shelf in the bathroom vanity is used to store hygiene products that are part of a family-based product **marketing** study.
- Section of kitchen used to explore kitchen **chemistry** experiments.
- Windowsill used to study effect of light on certain kinds of **plants**.
- Bedroom corner used to study **painting and sculpture**.
- Spare bedroom used to produce **theatrical plays and television** programs.
- Garage used to build and test **machines**.
- Dining room used (in non-dining hours) to create

and experiment with **floral arranging**.

- Walk-in closet used as a **journalism** workshop.

The learning center is a tangible statement to the child that her intellectual-creative pursuits have value and should be explored, and that the entire family supports her. Dedicating a part of your home for this purpose, no matter how small or large the space, is a powerful way of investing in your child's personal vision and life plan.

> If you would like guidance, tips and detailed steps for designing, setting up and maintaining a home learning center, see the workbook companion to this book: *The Three P's of Parenting: Family Workbook.*

We have now explored each of the three P's— power, protection and prediction—how they embody your child's needs, how she signals you when they are lacking, and how you can best respond. In the final section of this book, we will look at the practices of parents who have expanded upon the three P's to build highly effective communication with their children and lifelong, mutually supportive relationships.

Part Four

Redefining Parenthood

Chapter Nine
Parenting With Vision

We have taken a journey through the mind and motivations of your child. You have learned to recognize his behaviors and decipher his signals. Now, when he throws a tantrum, refuses dinner, or comes home late, you will know why, and you will know instinctively how to build a relationship that prevents those disagreeable behaviors by providing for his needs through thoughtful *pro*action.

Early in the book, I asked you to distance yourself from the parenting customs with which most of us are familiar, and to think in visionary ways about how to redefine the parent-child relationship with a clearer, more accurate understanding of what children seek.

Now, I would like to share with you approaches that were invented by parents to quell their reactionary tendencies with their children. We saw the effect of reactionary parenting in Chapter Two when we examined ways that discipline can sometimes perpetuate the behavior it is intended to correct.

Reactionary parenting is based largely on the emotion that your child triggers in you and involves making up rules as you go. When a parent reacts to a child's behavior, the child is driving the dynamic, not the parent. Reactionary parenting may feel easier or more natural, but the consequence of it is usually a tug-of-war in your relationship and a disconnect that need not exist.

A proactive parent, on the other hand, actively gathers data about the child by observing patterns in his behavior, develops systems that proactively address a child's needs (so that the child does not feel compelled to act out to get those needs met), and opens up decision-making processes so that the child becomes more integrated into and mentored by the family. Let us take a closer look at the techniques associated with proactive parenting.

You will notice that these practices, like those we have covered already, require behavior that most of us are not accustomed to using with children. You may, again, feel it necessary to stretch beyond your comfort zone in order to open your mind to the possibilities that these practices hold for you and your child.

From Reaction to "Read Action"

It starts in the crib with loud wails designed to bring you front and center quickly, and continues for years as your child uses behavior to get what she wants from you, when she wants it. The programming begins before you have barely become acclimated to the job of parent.

To manage your instinctive responses to her behavior

requires self-control, and that requires practice. The longer you have been parenting, the more children you have, and the busier you are, the more challenging it is for you to avoid reacting to your child's behavior and begin to collect valuable data about it. So, take it slowly with baby steps and small, achievable goals.

Steps for Data Collection

Distance. When you react to your child's behavior, you are too close, emotionally, to it. There is nothing wrong with being close to your child, but your emotions are not the ideal base from which to manage her. Start by practicing emotional distance when you feel discord of any kind with your child.

Imagine your child inside a fishbowl, bubble or on the other side of a glass wall. You can hear her, but her words are muffled so that you focus on tone. You can see her, but you are not able to interact with her. She can see you, but she cannot make you react.

Take one step back. Put your hands behind your back or by your side. Slacken your facial muscles. Do not frown or smile. Do not speak. Assume a posture of neutrality. Just observe. Quiet your mind, no matter how "loud" the situation is.

There is no need to do this for an unreasonable amount of time. A few seconds here, a minute or two there, is enough. In that frame of time, you can observe quite a bit about a child.

The first few times you try this, seconds will feel like hours. You will feel a slight panic. Your child will look slightly befuddled. It is likely that she will intensify her behavior the first or second time you distance yourself, because her program is not working. It is similar to when the elevator does not come, or the computer does not respond. We push the button again and again. So, she may escalate the behavior.

In learning how to have this distance, you will find that your shift away from a reactionary approach will have an immediate impact on her behavior. When you do not respond to her program, she will, after the first or second episode, begin trying other tests to find a new program. Do not concern yourself with this. Just take it slowly, and practice observing her without reaction.

Gather Data. When you achieve even the slightest ability to distance yourself in a moment of discord with your child, begin collecting data about her behavior and your own. There are endless ways to collect this data. You can simply take mental notes, or you can invest time in more thorough documentation. The more investment you make, the greater your returns will be.

Consider maintaining a journal and periodically jotting down your observations. Purchase an audio recording device and capture your observations during or shortly after the experience. Have debriefing sessions with your spouse or partner. Ask a friend or family member to help you reflect on your child's behavior by interviewing you about it.

The idea is to gather information over a period of time, so that you can better understand your child's pattern of behavior and the contextual framework that supports it. Here is what to look for when you make your observations:

> *Body Language.* Posture. Facial expressions. Use of arms and hands. Is her overall message an aggressive one? A weak one? Does her body movement make you want to draw near or retreat?

Voice. How does your child's voice sound, and how does it make you feel?

Eyes. Is she staring at you (or the person she is addressing), or is she looking away? Children often watch to see how their parents will react to their behavior.

Words. Listen as if you are deciphering a code, because you are. What is being said, and what do you think it really means?

USING VIDEO OR AUDIO RECORDERS

If you have time and inclination, consider collecting data with a video or audio recorder stationed nearby or kept on hand, so that you can capture behavior as it plays out. While recording your interactions may sound a tad Machiavellian, there is no more objective and informative way to study the dynamics of your interactions with your child.

Dynamics. If siblings are involved, look for the dominator and the victim, the one who is goading or agitating, dissuading or protecting. Are there others present? How do you normally respond to this behavior?

Context. Just as important as the behavior itself is the context in which it occurs. Be as detailed as you can in noting the place, time and circumstances of the behavior. What happened just prior? What happened as a result? Is this unusual behavior or a regular occurrence? Does it only happen in the presence of a certain person? Does it hold true at school and at home?

If you have a spouse or partner, or if there are others who provide care for your child at home or elsewhere, ask them to record observations of their own. Because she must program each adult differently, your child probably has distinct relationships with each person that provides care for her. You will benefit from seeing the distinctions, as well as the patterns, revealed by your child's interactions with other caregivers.

Identify Patterns. Once you have recorded 10-20 observations, take some quiet time to identify patterns. When does discord typically happen? What forms does it most often take? What are the circumstances? If you do not immediately see patterns in your data, continue collecting over a longer period of time.

Compare notes with your partner or spouse and with others that provide care and supervision of your child. Try to narrow the behaviors you see your child repeating to three or four essential ones that you can work with to create a healthier dynamic.

SYSTEMS

Most families have dozens of systems, but are unaware of them because those systems evolved organically over time. Your family may have a particular way of having dinner on weekday evenings, or a routine for getting everyone out of the house in the morning, or a ritual for hosting relatives when they visit, or a manner of celebrating certain traditions. Each of these is an unconscious choreography shaped by actions and reactions.

However, you also have the ability to design systems to address problems or enhance the functioning of your family. Throughout this book, I have shared system designs used successfully by other parents, from the simple system of managing a shared bathroom, to the more complex system of constructing a family policy.

When I ask parents what makes their systems work, nearly all mention the following factors:

1. Include your children. Even Lunchbox Age children are capable of gathering data about the family's dynamic and participating constructively in family discussions about systems. "You will find," said one parent, "that children offer a sincerity, candor and purity of perspective that will make your decisions better."

2. Build consensus. Healthy debate and negotiation among family members are a must, but consensus is only possible if there is firm, democratic leadership by the parents.

3. Start small and build. It cannot be said enough: take it slow. Every parent I have asked about system design emphasized how important it is to build a new practice slowly, in small steps that build on each other. For example, if you want to address an anger-protection cycle such as that discussed in Chapter Four, you might begin by simply practicing relaxation discipline for several weeks or months until you develop comfort with the practice. Then, you might introduce another technique, such as role play once a month to address the behavior that makes you angry. Gradually, you can expand your system to include scheduled attention that soothes your child and prevents her from provoking your anger.

You may not feel that you have addressed the problem, but one small change breaks the cycle, and from there, you can introduce other techniques until you have reshaped the behavior.

OPEN PROCESSES

What stops most parents from trying new approaches with their children is the fear of making mistakes and appearing clumsy and uncertain. Parenting requires a certain fearlessness, because every day you must make decisions, and every decision could be the wrong one.

Your fearlessness inspires your children to strive and take healthy risks. Your child gains more value from seeing you try—and sometimes fail—than from seeing only polished performances. So, while it may feel counterintuitive, the quickest way to earn your child's respect and capture her attention is through an honest and revealing dialogue about your decisions.

Transparency is challenging for parents because to achieve it, you must expose your decision-making process—your goals, intentions, fears, motivations, doubts and assumptions—to your child. Parenting usually involves secrecy. Parents make decisions in isolation, and children are informed only on a need-to-know basis.

Transparency, in contrast, involves bringing your child into the inner sphere of your decision-making process, not only so that she can see and learn from it, but so that she can also inform it. Many parents find it chilling to think of being transparent to their children, for fear that revealing their uncertainties will undermine their parental authority.

If you are completely honest and open with your child, do you relinquish power to her? No, but it feels that way, because we live with the illusion that by keeping children in the dark, we maintain control of their thoughts and feelings and protect them from worry.

In fact, concealing our doubts and designs limits us, forcing us to maintain a façade that distances us from our children, rather than bringing us closer to them.

In concealing our practices, we deny children the opportunity to learn those practices for themselves.

Take a moment to recall your own childhood. How were decisions made in your family? Was it an open or a closed process? If it was open, you participated in discussions about decisions that would ultimately impact you, before those decisions were made.

When you use an open process with your child, then before making a decision that will impact her, you:

- discuss your initial, raw thoughts about it with your child and with any other decision-making adult in the household *before* you come to a decision;
- share your fears, motivations, and convictions with your child; and
- invite your child's honest reactions.

When you have a process like this, you are modeling the elements of decision-making—skills that impact your child's sense of self, power, confidence, justice and freedom. You are also demonstrating the human element—the fact that decisions are made by people, that opinions vary, that humans are fallible, and that all decisions are not perfect ones. No decision is made without some measure of uncertainty and "what could have been."

If you grew up in a household with closed processes, you are uncomfortable with this uncertainty, sometimes to the point of inaction. Your parents made decisions decisively, instinctively, without letting you see their argument or dissension; and because you saw the outcome and not the process, you may believe that they were better equipped than you to parent. They may have appeared to be smooth operators, but there were undoubtedly messy mechanics behind their decisions.

The effect of being raised in a closed process is a lasting one. This approach trains us to keep decision-making quiet and prevent stakeholders (children, parents, spouses, friends, lovers, colleagues) from taking part. Closed processes are guided by assumptions, many of which can be wrong; and wrong assumptions can lead to miscommunication and dysfunctional relationships.

Open processes are guided by deliberation and invoke participatory democracy. Children who have been included in the conversation will be more comfortable with a decision, regardless of its outcome.

When you attempt an open process for the first time, explain to your child (using examples, images, role-play and context if she is younger) that you are attempting something new that feels slightly uncomfortable. Explain what you are attempting to do and invite her support and suggestions.

You will find a stunningly rich and intimate relationship with your child when you invite her into your life as a supporter, cheerleader, advocate, and sympathizer. You can still be her immortal leader and protector, while occasionally relying on her for support. After all, rock stars occasionally fall into the arms of their fans. Don't you want the arms of your biggest fan extended for you?

THE GUIDE INSIDE YOU

The only parenting guide you truly need, you already have within you. Ultimately, you must parent within your comfort zone, driven by the mores of your culture and society, the expectations you inherently feel are appropriate for your child, and the decisions you must make moment by moment, based on the context of the situation. No one but you can make those decisions, and no one but you can know whether those decisions are the right ones.

Use this book to understand your child better, and to learn how to communicate better with her, so that your preferences, expectations, rules and requirements can be understood. She *wants* to understand and abide by them. She wants nothing more than to please you and partner with you. You can trust in that.

Chances are that you have read this book in search of certainty in the deeply uncertain practice of parenting. Chances are that you also have experienced discord or strife with your child, and what you really want is harmony based on mutual respect and acceptance.

Use this book to build that certainty and harmony through insight and vision. Allow yourself to imagine a parenting experience in which your child has no need to act out, because your approach anticipates every need she has, before she has it. She comes to know you as someone on whom she can rely, someone who sees into her deepest fears and insecurities and comforts them before she barely has a chance to experience them. She comes to know you as someone who invites her power, her yearning to grow and achieve, and her need to have an identity that is her own.

Then, allow yourself to imagine a world shaped by children reared with conscious parenting, rather than through primal tug-of-war—generations of children growing under the model of informed, anticipatory parenting, and carrying that model forward into their own relationships and drawing from it to make the parenting decisions that ultimately shape societies to come. It is a stirring and evolutionary vision, to say the least.

So, it is our decision. We can continue parenting based on how we were raised, using the fading societal framework of our own youth as a reference; or we can map the framework of the coming generation and lead our children as pioneers. The choice is entirely our own.

The Three P's

Communication Toolbox

Strategies and resources for
communicating with your child
at every age.

COMMUNICATING WITH YOUNGER CHILDREN

Most **Wobbly Age** children and some **Lunchbox Age** children struggle with using language to express how they feel and what they want. They simply have not had enough experience or practice to effectively communicate. However, their awkwardness with language does not indicate a lack of depth or sophistication; children just need the proper tools.

Once you introduce the following methods of communication into your relationship with your younger child, you will discover his true capacity for meaningful interactions with you and with others.

Books and Role-Play. Books promote intimacy and conversation at any age, but particularly with young children. If there is a particular problem you want to discuss with your child, visit the bookstore or library with him seeking children's books that address the topic. If there is no specific problem, try using any children's book that depicts and explores family relationships.

INCLUDING YOUR CHILD IN THE SEARCH

When you bring your child along on your search for books, and include him in your conversations with librarians or bookstore staff, you model how to find resources to solve a problem and how to ask questions to find what you are seeking. Most importantly, you inspire him to help you look or to suggest books that he likes. In doing so, you make him a partner in the process

---

To get the most from children's books, use them in role-play with your child. Invite him to assign roles from the story to the two of you and even to inanimate objects (i.e., dolls and stuffed animals) that you incorporate into each scene. You are in for an eye-opening (and fun) experience when you empower him to control the action of the story.

Children's books are effective tools for communicating with your younger child because they provide a common reference point for the two of you. Images and story contexts provide him with a basis for understanding an issue without having to rely on words. Freed from language, he can channel thoughts and feelings through the story and its characters. He will compare his own experiences to those of the characters in the story, and when he sees similarities, he will put words into the mouths of those characters to represent his views.

For example, if you are going through a divorce and are reading a story with your child about a family that is experiencing divorce, your child is likely to express his opinions or feelings by saying what the characters feel and think. He might say "Little Bear is sad that Daddy Bear is leaving." He will not ascribe those feelings to himself, or to you or your spouse. In essence, he will outsource feelings to the characters.

During this type of role-play, it is common for children to make statements and reveal thoughts that surprise, and even disturb, their parents. However, it is critical that you stay in character and do not react personally to what your child is saying. He is working through his feelings and learning that it is safe to do so with you.

Do not be surprised if, during reading or acting out a story, your child embellishes dramatically. No need to stay with the storyline; it is just a vehicle for communication. It is common for children, once they feel comfortable with this activity, to take over the plot and improvise it, often leaving the original story behind completely.

Drawing. Drawing together can achieve the same results as reading together. As you draw together, talk about the "story" you are creating, who the characters are and, most importantly, *why* they behave as they do. You will probably have difficulty recognizing some of your child's scrawl, and you may also find it challenging to follow your child's train of thought as he constantly changes and redirects the storyline. Do not concern yourself with identifying figures or keeping the story straight. Your child is working through thoughts and feelings right in front of your eyes. Early drawing is a channeling mechanism for him to do this.

Focus on talking out the story with him as it is drawn. Rather than sitting and watching him work, draw alongside him while talking about your characters, what they are doing and, most importantly, what they are *feeling*. The more verbally engaged you are in this activity, the more motivated he will be to join you.

Listening. When you communicate with your child, your goal is to listen 90 percent of the time. In your next conversation with him, notice who speaks more, how you ask questions, how your child asks questions, and how you respond. Consider tape recording your conversation, showing your child the recorder and sharing your intent. You will probably be surprised by the way you talk with your child and the subtle dynamics of your interactions.

Signs and Signals. Language is generally your child's weakest communication tool. In addition, children are easily intimidated by confrontation. So, how can you encourage your child to come to you if he experiences a conflict? Establish a signal system for him to use to advise you of a problem without having to articulate or confront it.

For example, your child may be fearful of a bully in school, have anxiety about a declining grade in math, or feel uncertain about your relationship with your spouse or partner. These are difficult subjects for your child to address, but if he has the option of hanging a sign (such as a red square or a symbol of urgency) on his door or in a common area of the house to indicate that there is a problem, then you will know to initiate the conversation that opens a communication pathway for him.

Hand signals provide a way for children to communicate needs or feelings in the heat of the moment and without words. This tool is useful in sibling conflicts, interactions with you in public places, family meetings, and the like. I recommend that you take time for you and your child to explore a few useful phrases in sign language; however, if you do not have time to dedicate to this, work with your child to invent your own hand signals.

RESOURCES FOR COMMUNICATING WITH YOUNGER CHILDREN

Below are some recommended resources for communicating with your **Wobbly** or **Lunchbox Age** child. A complete list can be found in the supplement to this text, *The Three P's of Parenting: Family Workbook.*

OVERALL TOPICAL INDEXES

Literature indexes are valuable resources for parents because they can be searched by topic, author, illustrator or title. Here are two indexes of children's literature used widely by librarians, teachers and parents.

A to Zoo: Subject Access to Children's Picture Books, by Carolyn W. Lima and John A. Lima. (lists books appropriate for children in preschool through second grade).

Best Books for Children: Preschool Through Grade 6, by Catherine Barr and John T. Gillespie.

BULLYING AND FRIENDSHIPS

Picture Books
Ant Bully by John Nickle (also made into a movie)
Stand Tall, Molly Lou Melon by Patty Lovell
My Secret Bully by Trudy Ludwig
King of the Playground by Phyllis Reynolds Naylor
How to Be Cool in the Third Grade by Betsy Duffey

Nonfiction Books
Stop Picking On Me by Pat Thomas
Is It Right to Fight? A First Look At Anger by Pat Thomas
When Kids Drive Kids Crazy: How to Get Along With Your Friends and Enemies by Eda LeShan

Internet Resources
Getting Along with Groark at Live Wire Media (www.livewiremedia.com)

TALKING ABOUT DEATH

Picture Books
Lifetimes by Bryan Mellonie
A Dog Like Jack by Dyanne Disalvo Ryan
Grandma's Purple Flowers by Adjoa J. Burrowes
The Two of Them by Aliki

Nonfiction
I Miss You: A First Look At Death by Pat Thomas

Nonfiction for Adults
Talking With Children About Loss by Maria Trozzi

TALKING ABOUT DIVORCE

Picture Books
Dinosaurs Divorce!: A Guide for Changing Families by Marc Brown and Laurie Krasny Brown
Two Homes by Claire Masurel
My Family's Changing by Pat Thomas
What It the Chocolate Pudding?: A Story for Little Kids About Divorce by Sandra Levins

Nonfiction
The Kids' Book of Divorce: By, For, and About Kids by Fayerweather Street School Unit and Eric E. Rofes

Nonfiction for Adults
Megan's Book of Divorce: A Kid's Book for Adults by Erica Jong

TALKING ABOUT ADOPTION

Picture Books
The Day We Met You by Phoebe Koehler
I Don't Have Your Eyes by Carrie A. Kitze
Tell Me Again About the Night I Was Born by Jamie Lee Curtis

Nonfiction
Kids Like Me in China by Ying Ying Fry, Amy Klatzkin, Brian Boyd and Terry Fry

Nonfiction for Adults
Twenty Things Adopted Kids Wish Their Adoptive Parents Knew by Sherrie Eldridge
All About Adoption: How Families Are Made & How Kids Feel About It by Marc A. Nemiroff and Jane Annunziata

PREPARING FOR FIRST EXPERIENCES

Picture Books
First Experience Books (i.e., doctor, airplane, school) by Usborne
I Am Too Absolutely Small for School by Lauren Child
When You Go to Kindergarten by James Howe
Time to See the Doctor by Heather Maisner
What to Expect When the Baby Sitter Comes by Heidi Murkoff
What to Expect When You Use the Potty by Heidi Murkoff

TALKING ABOUT PREDATORS

Picture Books
Who Is a Stranger and What Should I Do? by Linda Walvoord Girard
The Right Touch: A Read-Aloud Story to Help Prevent Child Sexual Abuse by Sandy Kleven

Nonfiction for Adults
How to Protect Your Children on the Internet: A Road Map for Parents and Teachers by Gregory S. Smith

Internet & Video Resources
Stranger Safety DVD by Angela Shelton & John Walsh
NetSmartz (children) www.netsmartz.org

COMMUNICATING WITH OLDER CHILDREN

Children of **Telephone Age** respond best to communication that allows them to express themselves in private (such as journaling) or through escape into the fictional stories of other children their age, or by participating in democratic processes, like family meetings, where they can voice their opinions.

To maximize communication with your **Telephone Age** child, try the techniques and resources provided below:

Journal. As your child matures, he will pay less attention to you and more attention to his peers, and in doing so, he will become more private about his thoughts and feelings. Most parents notice their children turning increasingly to diaries and journals as they approach their tweens and teens. Private journals provide children with much-needed outlets for expression during this transitional phase when they no longer wish to confide in you and are not secure enough to confide in others.

Use the appeal of journaling to your advantage. Offer to keep a journal of your own and to keep it in a place that only your child can access. In your journal, to the extent that you are comfortable, model the communication you would like to see from your child by sharing your thoughts about difficult topics, your fears and concerns, your hopes and ambitions. Write as though you are confiding in your journal, not in your child, to keep the communication safely indirect.

While it is not appropriate to ask to see your child's journal, by sharing yours, you are providing a strong incentive for him to reciprocate. If he does reciprocate, read his journal, but make no comment about what he has written. Thank him for trusting you, and continue your practice of mutual confidence.

Movies. For older children, consider using movies (popular films or documentaries) to establish a common reference point for discussing a concern or challenge. For example, if you are going through a divorce, watch a movie together that portrays divorce and the experiences of a child in that situation. Your child is likely to recognize and identify with the movie's characters and to find comfort in seeing his own reality portrayed.

In watching the movie together, you are establishing a common context for later conversation, but do not expect that conversation to start immediately. You may find that your child does not comment on the movie or how it made him feel until days, or even weeks, afterwards. While younger children typically respond in the moment, older children need time to reflect and sort through their feelings before having the confidence to express them.

It is always best to include your child in the search for movies. Inquire together at a video rental store or look online. Then, have a movie night, and go out for ice cream afterwards so that you can take turns sharing your reactions to what you have seen. Do not push him to draw parallels between the movie and his personal experience. Limit your comments to the movie itself, analyzing, and inviting him to analyze, the actions and reactions of the characters.

Suggestion Box. Create a suggestion box where your child can submit concerns, questions, and, of course, suggestions. Consider addressing his submissions routinely as part of a family meeting or during a special outing for the two of you.

RESOURCES FOR COMMUNICATING WITH OLDER CHILDREN

Below are some recommended resources for communicating with your **Telephone Age** child. A complete list can be found in the supplement to this text, *The Three P's of Parenting: Family Workbook.*

TOPICAL INDEXES

Best Books for Children: Preschool Through Grade 6, by Catherine Barr and John T. Gillespie.

Best Books for Middle School and Junior High Readers: Grades 6-9, by John T. Gillespie.

Best Books for High School Readers: Grades 9-12, by John T. Gillespie.

BULLYING AND FRIENDSHIPS

Fiction
Indigo's Star by Hilary McKay
My Brother is a Superhero by Dyan Sheldon
Boy Proof by Cecil Castellucci
The Misfits by James Howe

Nonfiction
Difficult People: Dealing With Almost Anyone by Jennifer Rozines Roy

Internet & Video Resources
Stop Bullying Now at www.stopbullyingnow.hrsa.gov
Reality Matters by Discovery Channel at www.livewiremedia.com
Odd Girl Out by Lifetime TV at www.lifetimetv.com

TALKING ABOUT DEATH

Fiction
The Truth About Forever by Sarah Dessen

Stone Water by Barbara Snow Gilbert
The Outsiders by S. E. Hinton

Nonfiction for Children
Healing Your Grieving Heart for Teens: 100 Practical Ideas by Alan D. Wolfelt, Ph.D.

Nonfiction for Adults
Helping Teens Cope with Death by Dougy Center for Grieving Children

TALKING ABOUT DIVORCE

Fiction
Tuna Fish Thanksgiving by Carole S. Adler
To Live a Lie by Anne Alexander
The Top-Secret Journal of Fiona Claire Jardin by Robin Cruise

Nonfiction for Children
The Divorce Helpbook for Teens by Cynthia MacGregor

Nonfiction for Adults (see listings for younger children)

Popular Movies
Bye Bye Love (DVD)
Stepmom (DVD)

ADOPTION

Fiction
What I Call Life by Jill Wolfson
Find a Stranger, Say Goodbye by Lois Lowry

Nonfiction for Children
Who Am I? And Other Questions of Adopted Kids by Charlene C. Giannetti

Nonfiction for Adults
Beneath the Mask: Understanding Adopted Teens by Debbie Riley and John M.D. Meeks

Popular Movies
Meet the Robinsons (DVD)

PREDATORS

Nonfiction for Children
MySpace Safety: 51 Tips for Teens and Parents by Kevin M. Farnham

Nonfiction for Adults
Totally Wired: What Teens and Tweens Are Really Doing Online by Anastasia Goodstein
Cyber-Safe Kids, Cyber-Savvy Teens: Helping Young People Learn to Use the Internet Safely and Responsibly by Nancy E. Willard

Internet & Video Resources
Internet Safety DVD by Angela Shelton & John Walsh
2 SMRT 4U at www.2smrt4u.com
NetSmartz411 (adults) at www.netsmartz411.org

RESOURCES FOR COMMUNICATING WITH CHILDREN OF ALL AGES

School Library Journal (www.slj.com). An international reviewer of books, multimedia, and technology for children and teens.

PBS Kids It's My Life. (http://pbskids.org/itsmylife) Provides videos by and about children of all ages on the topics of friends, family, school, body, emotion and money.

Discovery Channel's COSMEO. (www.cosmeo.com) In addition to homework help, this resource provides videos and live support for personal challenges faced in school, such as bullying.

About LearnGarden

LearnGarden, Inc. is a company dedicated to parents. We empower parents who seek solutions to academic, emotional, developmental or social problems that arise in the lives of their children, ages 0-18. We provide practical advice and proven applications in personalized training sessions, small- and large-group workshops, and in private consultations.

We train parents to recognize and solve parenting problems with simple, effective techniques. As a companion service to our parent programming, we train children, ages 8-18, in the independent use of at-home approaches to overcoming the hurdles of school, life transitions and family relationships.

LearnGarden is based on the belief that the family and home environment are the most powerful influences on a child's growth and maturation. Our services support the goals of individual families as well as those of schools, corporations, community organizations and other institutions desiring to strengthen families and support more effective parenting techniques.

LearnGarden also embraces partnerships with product and service providers whose missions are driven by the desire to empower and support parents as the lead advocates for the success of their children.

The Three P's of Parenting

FAMILY WORKBOOK

The *Family Workbook* provides step-by-step guidance for parents and caregivers who wish to implement the principles and techniques introduced in *The Three P's of Parenting*.

The workbook includes advice and instruction on: designing a family policy, conducting family meetings, building consensus with children, designing schedules and routines, and planning and communicating about the future. Plus, you will find instructions for continuing the life planning process for children 12 and older.

The *Family Workbook* also includes sections designed specifically to involve your children, with age-appropriate activities that support their involvement in the building of a better family.

Visit LearnGarden at www.LearnGarden.com
to order your copy of the *Family Workbook* today.

Index

ABOUT THE AUTHOR

JENNIFER JONES, Ph.D., is the founder and CEO of Learn-Garden, Inc. and a specialist in learning and child development. Through her roles as workshop facilitator, public speaker, and private consultant, Dr. Jones has worked with hundreds of parents and thousands of teachers in the United States and abroad. A dy-  namic speaker, Dr. Jones delivers presentations with insights and discoveries that energize parents about the power and potential of children.

Dr. Jones holds a Master's and Ph.D. from Columbia University Teachers College. In addition to her experience in training parents and teachers, she has served as a university professor, participated in the design, development and management of ten schools (both public and private) and collaborated in local, regional and national studies on curriculum and learning. She has consulted for such organizations as the Young Presidents' Organization, the Corporation for Public Broadcasting, the Annenberg Foundation, Visa International, Jamaica's Ministry of Education, Argentina's Ministry of Education, Puerto Rico's Department of Education, Columbia University, Florida International University and Miami-Dade County Public Schools, among others.